Growing Better Vegetables

Growing Better Vegetables
A Guide for Tropical Gardeners

T. M. Greensill, M.B.E.

Evans Brothers Limited

Published by Evans Brothers Limited
Montague House, Russell Square, London, W.C.1.

First Published 1968
© T. M. Greensill 1968

Set in 11pt. on 12pt. Baskerville and printed
in Great Britain by Cox & Wyman Ltd,
London, Reading and Fakenham

237 49510 4   PR 4790

Contents

Section I. Preparation   *Page*

Chapter 1	Why do we want to grow our own vegetables?	9
Chapter 2	The tools for the job	11
Chapter 3	Feeding the plants	14
Chapter 4	Preparing the ground	23
Chapter 5	Buying, storing and planting seed	26
Chapter 6	Fighting pests and diseases	29
Chapter 7	How location, altitude and rainfall will affect the vegetables	35

Section II. Beans, Peas and Pulses

Chapter 1	French, Scarlet Runner and Lima Beans	38
Chapter 2	The Winged and Sword Beans	42
Chapter 3	Cowpeas and Garden Peas, including Catjang and Asparagus Bean	45
Chapter 4	Other interesting Beans and Peas. Bonavist Bean, Mung Bean, Soy Bean, Cluster Bean, Groundnut and Bambarra Groundnut	49
Chapter 5	Pests and diseases of the crops	54

Section III. Tomatoes, Garden Egg, Peppers and Gourds

Chapter 1	Tomatoes	59

		Page
Chapter 2	Garden Egg, Bird, Cherry, Cayenne and Sweet Peppers	64
Chapter 3	Ridge and English Cucumbers	69
Chapter 4	Watermelon and Musk Melon	72
Chapter 5	Okra and Chayote	74
Chapter 6	Pumpkins, Squash and Marrows	77
Chapter 7	Other interesting Gourds. Fluted Pumpkin, Chinese Preserving Melon, Bottle Gourd, Snake Gourd, Luffa, Bitter Melon	88
Chapter 8	Common pests and diseases of these crops	100

Section IV. Roots, Tubers and Bulbs

Chapter 1	Yams, Potatoes and Artichokes	107
Chapter 2	Carrots, Beetroot, White Turnip and Radish	112
Chapter 3	Onions, Leeks and Shallots	117
Chapter 4	Other interesting Root vegetables. Salsify, Scorzonera, Chinese Artichoke, Eddo, and Tannia	122
Chapter 5	Pests and diseases of these crops	125

Section V. The Leaf and Stem Vegetables

Chapter 1	Cabbage and Cauliflowers, including Collard, Scotch Kale, Couve Tronchuda, Celery Cabbage, Chinese Cabbage and Kohl-Rabi	129
Chapter 2	The Spinaches, including English Spinach, New Zealand Spinach, Indian Spinach, African Spinach and Chard	135
Chapter 3	Lettuce, Endive and Cress, including Land Cress, Indian Cress and Watercress	138

Chapter 4	Other interesting Leaf and Stem vegetables. Celery, Celeriac, Purslane, Water Leaf and Asparagus	*Page* 142
Chapter 5	Pests and diseases of these crops	146

Section VI. Culinary Herbs

Chapter 1	Basil, Chervil, Chives, Dill, Fennel, Garlic, Ginger, Marjoram, Mint, Parsley, Rosemary, Sage, Thyme	149
Index		157

List of Photographs

	Page
Selection of Tropical Vegetables	81
Basket of Tomato seedlings	82
French Climbing Bean – 'Kentucky Wonder'	82
Pole Lima Bean	82
Winged Beans	83
Bonavist Bean	84
Nematodes on bean shoots	84
Symptoms of virus disease on Lima Bean	84
Applying fertiliser to Tomato plants	85
Tying up Tomato plants	85
Garden Egg of the large round-oval type	86
Leaf Miner attack on Tomato leaves	86
Downy Mildew on Cucumber	87
Okra Perkin's 'Long Pod'	87
Pickleworm damage to Cucumber fruit	88
Tomato 'Dwarf Gem'	88
Fluted Pumpkin	89
Young Cucumber plants of the Ridge type	89
Making a Drill	90
Thrip damage on Onion leaves	91
Beetroot 'Deep Blood-red Globe'	91
Tannia	92
Water Leaf	92
Cabbage 'Jersey Wakefield'	93
Bed of Collard	94
Cauliflower 'Early Patna'	94
Chard	95
New Zealand Spinach	96
Downy Mildew on Lettuce	96
Symptoms of Black Rot on Cabbage leaf	96
Blue Scotch Kale	96

I. PREPARATION

Chapter 1 WHY DO WE WANT TO GROW OUR OWN VEGETABLES?

There are three very good reasons for doing so. Home grown vegetables are fresh, they are cheap and we get a real sense of achievement in producing them.

The freshness of vegetables grown in one's own garden and harvested when required is of first importance. Even with the most highly organised methods of transport, this freshness cannot be maintained and produce comes to the shop or market without its first crispness or 'bloom'. This is a loss, not only in appearance but in food value. The green outer leaves of lettuce or cabbage, for example, contain an abundance of vitamins and minerals, but the retailer does not think of this when he removes them in an attempt to freshen up his jaded produce. These vitamins and minerals are known as protective foods as they actively help the body to ward off disease, and are therefore an important part of our diet. It is not sufficiently recognised that the food value of any green vegetable is at its peak when first cut and that this food value diminishes as the leaves wilt. Take another case. The tomato picked fully-ripe from the plant and warm from the sun has a different taste and appearance from those picked underripe in order that they can survive their journey through many hands to their ultimate destination in the kitchen. At best these will have lost only the lovely bloom, but generally the skin will have toughened, they may be bruised and will have lost a great deal of their true flavour.

Cheapness. There can be no question but that it is cheaper to grow one's own vegetables. Let us take the tomato as our first example. For an expenditure of roughly one shilling for seed and two shillings for fertiliser, a bed of twenty-five plants properly grown will produce anything from fifty to seventy-five pounds of fruit. Again, an ounce of cabbage seed costing in the region of five shillings should produce about six thousand plants—rather more than the average householder needs, but this serves as an indication of the vast difference between the cost of the home grown and the retailed product. There are many other prolific vegetables which will prove just as rewarding if carefully grown—the French bean, lettuce and garden egg are the first to spring to mind. Such vegetables as carrot, turnip and beetroot are doubly valuable as they not only produce edible roots but edible foliage also of high dietetic value. When retailed these tops are either discarded or sold separately. The home grower can harvest this additional crop at no extra expense. Lastly, he can usually dispose profitably of any vegetables surplus to his own requirements.

Freshness and cost are obvious practical advantages, readily appreciated by all. But the joy of harvesting the fruits of one's labours and the sense of achievement it brings is personal to the gardener himself.

Now, having decided that a vegetable garden is a very desirable thing, we must face the fact that a successful one needs very careful planning. To get the maximum return we must know (1) what vegetables will do best in our particular locality and soil, (2) how long they will take to mature so that we can plan a continuous supply, (3) what fertilisers and manures to use, and (4) how to deal with those pests and diseases that bedevil the gardener wherever he is.

In the following chapters an attempt has been made to tackle these problems in non-technical language. Even in the most difficult terrain, good vegetables can and have been produced where the desire to create a garden has been combined with an understanding of the difficulties involved.

Chapter 2 THE TOOLS FOR THE JOB

Although excellent crops can be produced with only a native-type hoe and a machette, it is far easier to do the work with the correct tools. The beginner will need only a few basic tools but, as all gardeners tend to collect more and more over the years, a fairly extensive range of tools and equipment will be described. In all cases, do buy the best you can possibly afford as cheap tools rarely give good service, being either badly made or of poor quality material.

For any work in the garden, the basic requirements are a digging fork, spade, rake, hoe, watering can and a few shallow, locally made baskets or wooden trays for seed boxes.

The standard garden fork can be obtained in four sizes; when buying, it is as well to consider the weight carefully, choosing the one you can use without too much exertion. A fork which is too heavy can make work very arduous and in all probability a job will take longer than if a lighter fork were used. Fork tines are usually made rounded or square; there is, however, a special type with flat broad tines for use when turning compost or manure, as the flat tines make it easier to pick up the material.

Spades are almost universally one shape—oblong, and must not be confused with shovels, which are no use for digging. Cheap steel will often bend or crack if the work is heavy, so it is essential to buy a good one, preferably of an established brand. If supplies of tools are hard to come by or if you live a distance from a town, it is as well to buy an extra handle, as handles have an unhappy knack of breaking just when the work is urgent.

A good rake is essential too, not only for raking the soil down before planting small seeds but also for gathering up weedings and rubbish: it will save a lot of back bending. Again, a strong one is to be preferred.

Hoes come in different shapes for different uses. A 5" or 6" Draw hoe is extremely useful for cultivation between rows of vegetables. The Dutch or Push hoe cuts off weeds when it is pushed through the soil just below the surface. It is desirable to have one of each.

Watering cans can be had in great variety. The only ones really essential are a small one fitted with a very fine rose for watering young seedlings, and a large one for watering the plants in the beds. With beds that are deeply mulched, watering with buckets can be quite satisfactory if one doesn't want to go to the expense of buying a large watering can.

To list all the additional tools and equipment you might like to have would be rather a long job, so let us confine ourselves to the more reasonable items. You must certainly provide yourself with some means of protection against pests and diseases. It is advisable to get suitable equipment for administering both powder and liquid insecticides and fungicides. There are a great many of both types to choose from and they range from the simple to the complicated.

By far the simplest way of applying a dust to a small crop is to put the dust in a square of fairly coarse-weave material such as linen. Take all four corners in the hand and tie round, leaving a little space between the string and the powder. The dust is then directed at the plant with a sharp jabbing motion, stopping short of the plant by a few inches. The dust will be forced through the spaces of the woven material and scattered evenly over the plant. If larger areas are to be dusted, you may like to invest in one of the simple dusters which employ a bellows to blow out the dust. Another type is worked by turning a handle. Both are inexpensive and well worth the money.

With liquid sprays, the object is to deposit a very fine mist all over the plants to be treated. Unless the mist is very fine, the droplets tend to amalgamate and run off the leaves to the ground, wasting a lot of the liquid. It is for this reason that application by a fine-rosed watering can is so wasteful. Most liquid sprayers have a nozzle which can be adjusted to give a fine mist, ensuring an overall fine deposit on the plants. The 'bicycle-pump' type of spray is one of the most popular. It is cheap, easy to handle and maintain. It is used with a bucket containing the mixed liquid. This liquid is sucked up by the pump through a plastic or rubber tube and forced out of the nozzle.

Pressure sprayers are more suitable where there is a great deal of spraying to be done. The liquid is placed in a plastic or metal container, which is then closed with an airtight stopper. A pump attachment is used to raise the pressure inside the container, and as soon as the outlet is opened a spray is sent out which continues until the pressure inside the container falls. This is the most convenient of all the smaller types of spraying equipment. The new ones with plastic containers are very light and easy to move about.

Thinking in terms of moving things about, I do think a wheelbarrow is a good investment. So much labour will be saved in the carting of compost and collection of rubbish and composting materials. Small metal ones are far more convenient than the heavier wooden ones; those fitted with rubber tyres are very easy to use, particularly over uneven ground.

With all tools and equipment, a little time spent in cleaning them well after use will pay dividends. Tools such as spades and forks should be washed and dried and then wiped with an oily rag. Digging with a spade caked with several pounds of dirt not only adds to the labour but rusts the metal. Tools will last longer if oiled and hung up after use.

The easiest way to clean liquid sprayers is to pump clean water through them. This will dislodge all the chemicals in the nozzle and keep it free

Obviously, when the same sprayer has to be used for all types of sprays, absolute cleanliness is essential. A residue of the wrong chemical can damage a crop. This is dealt with more fully in later chapters.

Chapter 3 FEEDING THE PLANTS

Under-nourishment is the cause of many failures in vegetable growing. To ensure that your crops do not fail because they have not received sufficient nourishment, it is first necessary to understand how the plant gets its food and what the food requirements are of some of our main crops.

Most plants obtain some of their food from the air and the rest from the soil. The gas, carbon dioxide, which is in the air, is absorbed by plant foliage and, by the action of sunlight and chlorophyll (the green colouring matter in the foliage) processed in the leaves to produce complex sugars. These sugars are in turn changed into starches for the production of plant tissue. This process requires water, and this the plant draws up from the soil through its roots. In this water which the plant gets from the soil are many chemicals in solution, some of which are vitally necessary to the plant. It has been established that at least twelve chemicals are necessary to the health and growth of a plant: it is probable that further research will show that more than this number are essential.

Of these twelve known chemicals some, such as nitrogen, phosphorus, potash, calcium, sulphur and iron are needed by the plant in relatively large quantities, whilst others, such as molybdenum, are needed only in minute amounts. A very rich soil would probably have enough of these chemicals to satisfy plant needs, but very rich soils are the exception, not the rule. But to get high yields from our vegetables, most soils need to be enriched to meet the demands of highly productive plants. Different vegetables need different mixtures of these chemicals, and details of these requirements are given later for each crop.

Extra supplies of essential chemicals can be applied to the soil in two forms—either as an organic manure (made by the breaking down of living matter), or as an inorganic manure or fertiliser (produced from a mined rock or as a by-product of industry). Both will be discussed in more detail later in the chapter. Here let us consider how plants take their food from the soil. As the plant can only absorb liquid through its roots, it follows that any nutriment must be capable of dissolving in the soil water. A plant cannot take in solid matter through its roots. Let us take as an example a common tropical soil type, laterite, which contains a lot of iron. This iron is in a form not readily soluble in water, so although a great deal is available, very little gets through to the plant. This starves the plant of the iron it requires and it will exhibit special symptoms of iron deficiency. In such a case, to make good this deficiency, we should have to apply sulphate of iron to the soil, since sulphate of iron dissolves readily in water.

So far we have only considered the soil as a source of chemical food for the plant. Now let us consider the soil itself. If the underlying rock from which your garden soil was derived is limestone, then your soil will be alkaline, as lime is an alkali. Some vegetables will thrive on an alkaline soil, while others demand an acid soil. Before, therefore, deciding on which plants you are going to grow, it is advisable to have your soil tested. This can be done quite simply, either through the Ministry of Agriculture, or by purchasing a small kit which will enable you to do it yourself.

The result of the test will be given as a symbol 'pH' followed by a number. This number may be as low as pH 4·0 for a very acid soil, or as high as pH 8·5 on a limestone soil (very alkaline). A neutral soil is expressed as pH 7·0. Your soil may be anywhere between pH 4·0 and pH 8·5. Fortunately, many of the vegetables mentioned in later chapters have a wide tolerance within this range. Some, however, are very particular, and their pH requirements are specifically stated where this is the case. To attempt to grow such plants in unsuitable soil is to ask for failure.

Whilst it is a very expensive matter to make a limestone soil more acid, it is an easy matter to make an acid soil more alkaline by the application of lime, thus making it more suitable for a wider variety of vegetables. This not only neutralises some of the acid in the soil, but also makes certain plant foods, such as potash, more readily available to the plant.

The amount of lime needed depends on whether the soil is sandy or clay. If sandy, between one and two pounds for every 100 square feet will usually be enough to alter the pH by 1·0, that is, say, from pH 4·5 to pH 5·5. If your soil is a heavy clay, however, you may need to apply as much as six pounds to every 100 square feet to get the same result.

When applying lime, fork it in to the top three inches of soil. If worked any deeper, much of its effect will be wasted as some will be drawn down to the lower stratas of the soil beyond the range of the roots of the plants. Never apply lime at the same time as organic manures, for chemical action may take place and reduce the value of both lime and manure.

COMPOST AND ANIMAL MANURES

So far we have thought of the soil only as a source of chemicals to be absorbed by the plant and enable it to grow well. But this is by no means all. A good soil is alive. It contains countless millions of living organisms, many of which are too small to be seen by the naked eye. This vast population is vital to the soil. By using the materials which make up the soil for their own food, they produce chemical and physical changes in the soil structure which are invaluable to plant growth. Without them, the soil would be inert and as capable of producing good vegetables as a heap of river sand.

To support this vast underground population, the presence of one material in sufficient quantity is essential, that is decayed and decaying vegetation, usually referred to as *humus*. On this essential decaying material some of the smallest of these organisms work, turning it into good black soil, rich in easily available plant foods. Under natural conditions such as high forest, there is an ample supply of decaying vegetation due to leaf fall and normal plant death. If we look under the leaves we shall find a layer of black crumbly material which has been produced by the soil organisms from fallen leaves and dead vegetation of previous years. Unfortunately, this condition does not obtain in our gardens and we have to make this valuable humus ourselves which, when matured, we call compost.

MAKING COMPOST

The importance of compost cannot be over-stressed. In many gardens in the tropics it is the only available source of organic manure. All experienced gardeners will confirm that the basic requirement of all garden plants is compost.

Fortunately the materials we need to produce compost are usually close at hand, since many of the waste materials from the garden can be turned into valuable plant-feeding material through the process of composting. The most suitable materials for the compost heap are grass cuttings from the lawn, hedge clippings, weeds, trimmings from vegetables used in the kitchen and any young growth. Older, tougher materials such as cabbage stems and woody branches can be used, but they will not disintegrate as quickly as the more succulent materials and may have to be processed twice.

In the composting process, all this green vegetative material gradually disintegrates. This disintegration comes about through the destructive action by minute bacteria on the tissues of the vegetation. By this action they change it physically and chemically into dark, crumbly compost. These tiny organisms or bacteria are to be found in rotting fruits, and so into the compost heap must go all the over-ripe fruits from the kitchen, as well as all the orange skins and pulp, paw-paw rinds, potato and yam peelings there are available. All these materials are known as 'starters' because they start the process of composting. Horse and cattle manure acts in the same way.

There are various ways of making compost, but the most usual is either to stack the materials in heaps or place them in trenches. In areas of high rainfall, the stack method is best, and the trench method is more suitable in areas of low rainfall or when making compost during the dry season. In both cases the process is essentially the same.

Let us start with the stack method. Here the materials are stacked to make convenient sized heaps, 4 feet square and up to 5 feet in height has proved most satisfactory for an average-sized garden. If sufficient material

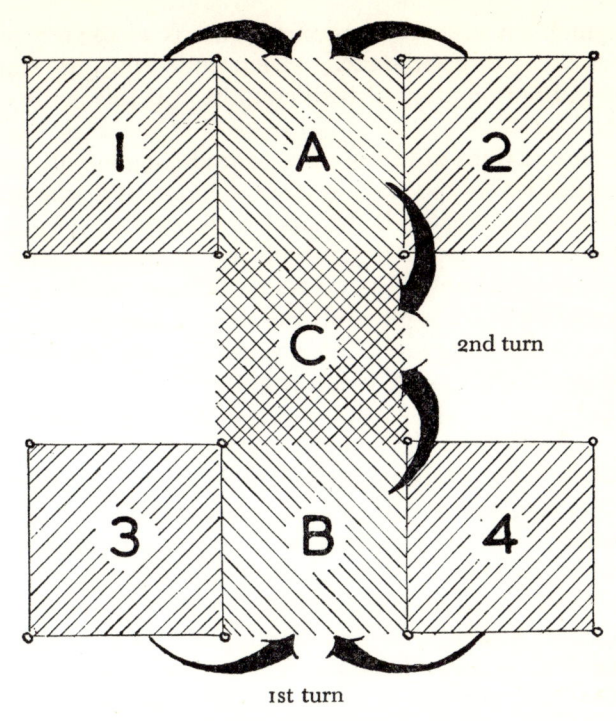

Fig. 1. Sequence of turning compost

is available, then four such stacks should be made at a time. The diagram above shows how the heaps should be turned, two heaps into one after about two weeks, and the resultant two heaps into one after a further two weeks.

During the rains in high rainfall areas when most of the compost will be made, it is advisable to lay sticks or bamboo poles on the sites first, before starting to make the heaps. This will ensure that the bottom layer does not become a nasty soggy mass which will not turn into compost.

Start the stacks from the outside, building up a 9" wall of grass cuttings or similar material. This wall prevents flies penetrating into the centre of the heap where they will find material on which to lay their eggs. If this should happen, the composting will become a nuisance to you and your neighbours. When the wall around the perimeter is finished, fill up the inside with any available materials, some of which must be the 'starters' mentioned earlier. When you have filled in to the height of the wall, continue by raising the wall a further 9", and again fill, continuing in this way until the stack is about 5 feet high. If it is not possible to finish a stack in a day, do see that the top is sealed either with grass, woodash or soil—again to stop the fly menace. Woodash can be used in the compost heap as well as for sealing, as it contains valuable potash.

As soon as the heap is finished, push a strong stake horizontally into the centre of one wall. The composting process produces heat, so that a few days after a stack has been made the temperature at the centre should rise, and this heats the end of the stake. When pulled out, the stake should be so hot that it cannot be grasped with comfort. If this is the case, then all is going well.

Except during periods of heavy rain, compost stacks will need watering. The temperature inside the stack is a clear indication whether or not the moisture content is correct. If the stack is either too wet or too dry, heat will not be generated and compost will not be made. So it is a matter which must be decided on the spot, when and how much water to give. If the materials in the stack are mainly young and succulent, then less water is needed than if the materials are older and the weather drier.

Stacks usually need turning twice at about 14-day intervals. Again, it is the temperature of the heap which determines the turning. The temperature inside the heap should rise to a peak after a week or ten days, and then start to fall. Here the stake which has been thrust into the heap will act as a thermometer. If, on removal, it is cool, then it is time to turn the heap so that the outside material is now placed into the centre of the new heap where it can be dealt with by the bacteria.

After the second turning, the compost should be properly broken down, but it should not be used until it has been given time to mature. During this maturing process it should be kept covered, for from now on the chemicals in the compost can easily be washed out. There will be no physical difference in the appearance of the material, but nonetheless it will have lost much of its value. So always keep your compost covered, protected from both sun and rain.

If you decide to use the trench method of making compost, you must first of all select a place in the garden which will not later become water logged in heavy rain. Dig the trench 4 feet wide and as deep and as long as you have available materials to fill it, allowing a few extra feet to play with so that the compost can be turned from one end of the trench to the other. Fill with compost materials in the same way as for the heap method, but here there is no need to build a wall of grass round the sides. Make sure that the top is well sealed from flies by finishing off with a layer of grass cuttings or an inch of soil or wood-ash. As soon as the temperature drops the compost material can be turned. This is generally within two or three weeks, dependent on weather conditions.

It is as well to work out roughly how much compost will be needed for the planting programme and try to make it during the rainy season, when succulent vegetation is readily available. As a rough guide, work on the basis of a minimum of 2 bushels of compost for every 100 square feet of bed to be planted. A bushel of compost at average moisture content weighs about 60 lbs.

There are many other valuable organic manures which can be used in the vegetable garden, and as some of them may be available in your locality the relative values of the commoner ones are considered below.

Horse and cattle manure are both of great value as they contain a wide range of chemicals and much valuable humus. Horse manure should be allowed to mature before it is used, for if used fresh the heat generated will damage roots. Cattle manure can be used fresh. Neither should be allowed to remain uncovered as the valuable chemicals can be leached out by sun and rain. Both manures will improve the soil. They assist sandy particles to form into crumbs and help to 'lighten' a heavy clay soil by improving drainage and aeration.

Sheep and Goat manure are also very useful. They can be used either fresh or mature. If stored, the manure must be covered of course. Their effect on soils is similar to the above, but often have a higher nitrogen content than cattle manure.

Poultry manure should be used with caution as it contains a high percentage of readily available nitrogen, which may have a bad effect on some crops. It can be very useful as a starter in compost making. This nitrogen is easily leached out, and once this has happened the remaining manure has little value.

Seaweed is rich in valuable chemicals and humus. Only true seaweed should be used, which is easily identifiable by its air bladders. Always allow seaweed to weather before use in order to get rid of the salt. Used fresh, it will damage some crops. Seaweed makes a valuable addition to the compost heap.

Sea grass, which is often found on beaches, is about 2 inches long and has no air bladders. It is low in chemicals and does not break down easily, and is therefore of little use.

Blood meal and dried blood can sometimes be obtained from Government-controlled slaughter houses. If it is not too expensive, it is an excellent source of nitrogen. It is particularly useful for leaf vegetables in those cases where a rapid increase in growth over a short period is needed. If allowed to get damp in storage, its value will be greatly reduced. It is best kept in wooden boxes.

Crushed bones and bone meal are valuable on acid soil as they supply phosphorus gradually over a long period. Bone meal has the more rapid action and is usually applied as a top dressing to give a crop an added boost of phosphatic manure.

Wood ash: Where wood is used for fuel, the ash should be stored for use on vegetable beds or incorporation into the compost heaps. Many tropical soils are known to be deficient in potash and an application of wood ash will be beneficial. Store very carefully, as even dampness will leach out the potash and the ash will be of little value.

Green manurings: For centuries, leafy crops have been grown specifically to dig back into the soil. Such leafy legumes as Mucuna, Calapogonium, Peuraria and Centrosema are of particular value on land temporarily vacant of crops. As soon as the plants produce flowers, they should be dug into the surface soil. When this leafy material has decomposed in the soil, it provides very valuable humus and many much-needed chemicals. During the process of decomposition, however, green manure tends to take nitrogen from the soil: it is therefore advisable to give a dressing of sulphate of ammonia or some similar nitrogenous fertiliser.

INORGANIC MANURES

So far we have discussed manures derived from living materials which add valuable plant foods and humus to the soil. These will change a soil physically and chemically, and this is of continuing benefit. Inorganic manures, commonly called 'fertilisers', do not add humus to the soil, but they can and do greatly increase the amount of plant food in the soil. The use of both types of manure in conjunction is strongly recommended.

In recent years there has been a great increase in the use of fertilisers in the tropics and much work has been done in Research Stations to find the best fertiliser treatment for local conditions. As fertiliser requirements of vegetables vary with the type of soil and climatic conditions, specific recommendations of a suitable mixture of fertiliser for each vegetable cannot be laid down here. But in most countries, this information can be obtained from the Ministry of Agriculture. We will, however, discuss the merits of the more generally available fertilisers, their main uses and their accepted standards of quality.

Fertiliser mixtures: In most countries, specially prepared mixtures are now available, either for specific crops or for a range of crops which have the same fertiliser requirement. It is fairly common practice to show the analysis of the fertiliser on the container, which is usually expressed as a ratio of three sets of figures. Let us take as an example 4:10:6. This mixture would contain 4% Nitrogen, 10% Phosphoric Acid and 6% Potash. A 100 lb. bag would therefore provide 20 lbs. of soluble foods of these three important chemicals, plus other useful chemicals which may or may not be stated on the container. From this example it will be seen that the higher the numbers, the more concentrated the fertiliser mixture, with a consequent increase in cost.

High analysis fertilisers are of great value in the tropics, once it is realised that it is more economical to make small applications at frequent intervals. There is a definite risk of loss with large applications, due to leaching out, particularly when rainfall is heavy.

Sulphate of Ammonia: A whitish powder produced as a by-product of the Coal Gas Industry, which is high in nitrogen. This is not immediately available to the plant; it has to be processed in the soil first, but in the tropics this only takes a few days. It is used as a top dressing for certain crops which need a boost when half grown, lettuce and cabbage being typical examples. Within ten days of an application there will be an increase in leaf growth and a darkening in the colour of the leaves. It is better to make two or three small applications rather than one large one, particularly in high rainfall areas, as any nitrogen salts the plant has not absorbed in a few days may be washed down beyond the reach of the roots. As sulphate of ammonia has a caustic effect on foliage, care should be taken to see that it does not touch the leaves of the plants.

It does have a tendency to make soils more acid and should be used with caution where the pH indicated that the soil is already markedly acid. On the other hand, it can be used on alkaline soils where this tendency is an advantage.

If allowed to get damp, much of its value will be lost, so it is advisable either to have only enough for immediate requirements or keep any not immediately required in wooden containers, raised off the ground.

Nitrate of Soda: Also called Chilean nitrate and saltpetre. Originally, this was all mined from nitrate beds in the deserts of Chile, but some is now produced synthetically.

Nitrate of soda is used only as a top dressing. It is more rapid in action than sulphate of ammonia and when rapid soft growth is required, this is the best fertiliser to use. Again, apply carefully so that it does not get on the leaves and burn them. In contrast to sulphate of ammonia, it leaves an alkaline deposit which makes it particularly valuable when used on an acid soil. On heavy clay soils, however, it should be used cautiously as it tends to make them even less easy to work. Store in the same way as sulphate of ammonia.

Nitrate of Ammonia, Nitrate of Potassium and Nitrate of Lime: These are all excellent nitrogenous fertilisers. Nitrate of ammonia contains up to 35% N, partly as nitrate and partly as ammonia. Nitrate of lime contains not only about 15% N as nitrate, but also 20% lime, and is therefore doubly valuable on acid soils. Its great disadvantage is that it readily absorbs water and is therefore extremely difficult to store. All three may be used in the same manner as nitrate of soda.

Superphosphate: A fine whitish-yellow powder produced commercially by the action of sulphuric acid on rock phosphate.

It is used extensively in mixed fertilisers, where it provides the phosphates, which are readily available to the plant. It is normally applied to the soil before planting as it aids root formation. It is also considered vital for the production of cells in the plant, to hasten maturity and improve the quality of the crop. Since most crops require comparatively large quantities of phosphates, it is particularly valuable in the tropics, where many soils cannot provide sufficient phosphate for vegetable production.

Superphosphate should not be applied at the same time as lime, where that is being applied to an acid soil, as much of its value will be lost because of chemical interaction—the phosphate would be changed into calcium phosphate, which is not soluble and is therefore useless to plants.

Basic slag: A grey powder produced as a by-product from steel manufacture. Dependent upon the process of manufacture, it may contain from 12% to 20% phosphates and a small percentage of free lime. Of value when applied to acid soils. The phosphates are made available quickly and in a condition that prevents them from being leached out easily. Neither superphosphate nor basic slag present any storage problem, but nonetheless they should be kept dry.

This should not be applied at the same time as organic manures or fertilisers containing ammonia, or there will be a chemical action which will reduce the value of both.

Sulphate of Potash: A powder produced from the raw chemical Kainit, mined in Germany. This is the purest type of potash fertiliser and is usually the most expensive.

Many tropical soils are deficient in potash, and since all parts of the plant need potash, this deficiency can prove serious. Although a full understanding of what use the plant makes of potash is not known, it is known that absence or shortage reduces the plants' resistance to disease. It can be used as a basic dressing before planting, and also as a top dressing.

It must be kept dry whilst in store, but does not easily leach out of the soil. On acid soils its action will be improved if used in conjunction with lime.

Muriate of Potash (Potassium Chloride): Similar to the above and can be used in the same way, but because of its chloride content is not always thought to be as good as sulphate of potash.

Chapter 4 PREPARING THE GROUND

There are two main methods of vegetable cultivation used by small growers—raised bench beds or sunken beds. Each has its own advantages and suitability to particular conditions.

The raised bench bed: This is probably the most widely used, particularly in areas of high rainfall. Beds are raised above the surface of the surrounding ground in order to improve the drainage and ensure that during heavy rains the vegetables are not flooded out.

It is usual to make paths between the beds, and the topsoil which has been removed from them is placed on top of the beds. These paths act as natural drainage channels in wet weather. The beds are sited across the slope of the land to minimize loss of soil by erosion. The diagram on page 24 illustrates this type of layout. It may be necessary to construct small crosschecks at points along the paths to check rushes of water and crosspaths should be staggered to prevent sudden rushes of water during heavy rain storms.

If enough water is available, during the dry season the paths can be used as irrigation channels.

Beds are usually made 4 feet wide, but may be of any length, although 25 feet is usually regarded as the most convenient length. Longer beds may give trouble during heavy rains in high rainfall areas when the paths fill with water. With no near outlet, the water may force a channel through the top soil of the beds, taking with it plants and soil.

The tops of the beds should be made to slope downwards from front to back, having the front facing the downward slope of the land. This will ensure that no soil is washed downhill. As a further precaution against erosion, clumps of grass planted along the front of the bed will help to stop the soil from crumbling away. Lemon grass is a favourite for this work, but any grass which grows in a small clump may be used. Creeping grasses should not be used as they will spread over the top of the bed and compete with the plants for food.

Sunken beds: These are mainly used where rainfall is low and moisture has to be conserved as much as possible. The beds are sunk from 3 to 6 inches below the surrounding paths and can follow the same pattern as the bench bed. This type of bed is easy to irrigate, either by hand or plastic or rubber hose.

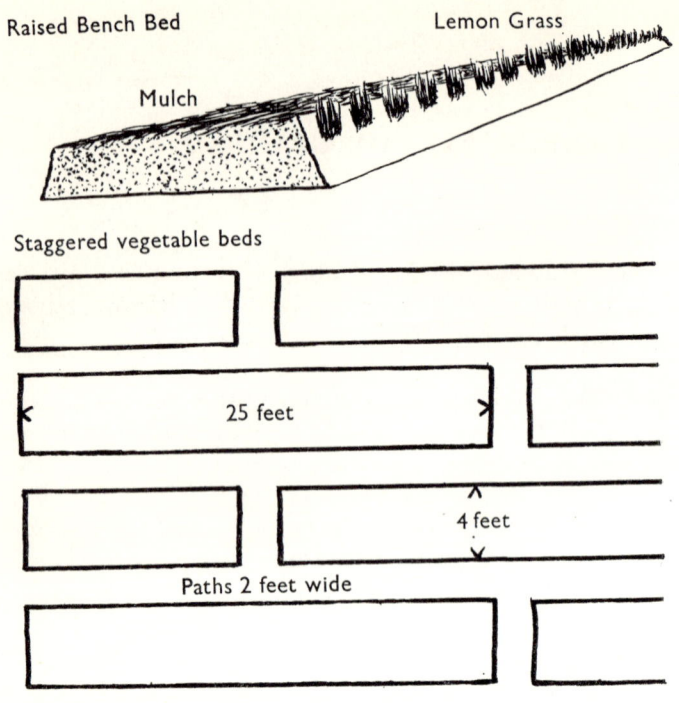

Fig. 2. Vegetable beds

PREPARATION OF THE LAND AND DOUBLE DIGGING

Having marked out whichever type of bed is most suitable for your location, the beds can now be prepared for planting. The soil needs to be well dug so that (1) all weed growth can be turned in; (2) more air can be introduced between the crumbs of the soil, which benefits the soil organisms; and (3) the larger lumps of soil can be broken down to allow the plant roots to penetrate more easily. When turning in weed growth, do not bury any that are carrying seeds or a fresh crop of weeds will appear in a few days.

It is very likely that the soil below the top few inches has not been disturbed for years, if ever, and such compacted soil presents a barrier to plant roots. This hard layer should be broken up, not only to allow roots ease of movement but also to improve drainage. This operation of breaking up a hard layer beneath the top-soil is known as 'double digging', and is essential to most tropical soils if high yields are required.

First of all remove an area of top-soil and place it on one side, exposing the slightly lighter coloured sub-soil, lighter in colour since it contains less humus. If this is very compacted it will have to be broken up with a pick, but usually a strong garden fork is adequate. Do not break it up too finely since there is a danger of it compacting again very quickly. Lumps of about 1 inch diameter are ideal. When this is done, expose the next area by turning the next top-soil back on to the sub-soil which has just been broken up. The diagram below illustrates this operation.

Once the soil has been double-dug, a too acid soil can be given an application of lime.

Where small seeds are to be sown direct into the bed, the top-soil must be broken down very finely and all lumps and stones removed.

MULCHING

The value of mulching cannot be stressed too much. It helps to keep the soil cool and retain moisture, thus enabling roots to function normally, even on the hottest days. It helps to prevent erosion of the valuable top-soil, weed growth is restricted and last, but not least, the mulch gradually rots down to form humus and enrich the soil. It may be of cut grass, leaves, rice husks, wood chippings or any type of vegetation that does not include ripe seeds. If using long grass, place it lengthwise along the beds as a further insurance against erosion.

It has been demonstrated conclusively that vegetables deeply mulched can be grown without shade, even at the hottest season of the year. There may be a temporary wilting at midday, but the plants revive in the afternoon.

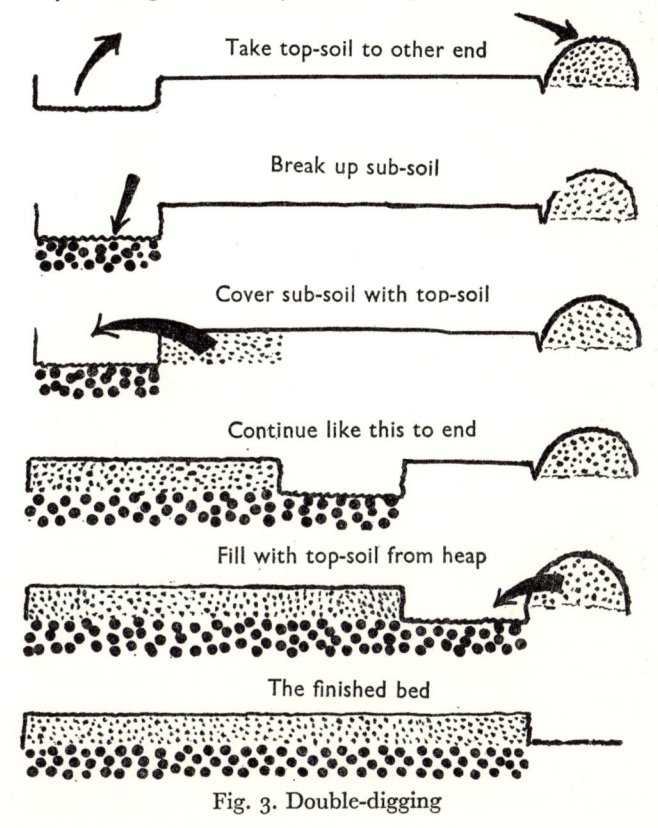

Take top-soil to other end

Break up sub-soil

Cover sub-soil with top-soil

Continue like this to end

Fill with top-soil from heap

The finished bed

Fig. 3. Double-digging

Chapter 5 BUYING, STORING AND PLANTING THE
          SEED

The choice of suitable seed is vital to success. Preferably, you should try to get seed that is fresh. As fresh seed is not always available, then you must get seed that has been properly stored and has not lost its viability (ability to germinate properly). Choose, too, a variety of the vegetable suitable to your locality.

Seed bought from reputable firms has been well stored, often now in metal foil. From such firms seed is usually guaranteed to be free from many of the serious diseases.

Particular emphasis must be laid on choosing a suitable variety. It is useless just to buy, say, tomatoes, when there are hundreds of varieties, most of which will not give good yields in the tropics. Try to get seed of a recognised tropical variety, or that has been known to do well in your locality.

If you are proposing to use your own seed or some from a local grower, do see that the seeds have been taken from plants showing no symptons of disease and harvested when fully ripe.

Viability, is often a difficult thing to ensure in the more humid tropics. Under moist conditions, badly stored seed will often begin to germinate during storage, despite the fact that the seed coat is not broken and there are no outward signs of germination. When seeds germinate in this way but do not break through the seed coat, the germ dies, although outwardly the seed appears to be normal.

Whatever seed you use, it is well worth while carrying out a germination test on each batch of seeds. For ordinary purposes, a sample test involving a few seeds is all that is necessary. Take ten or so seeds at random and place them on dampened blotting paper, cut to fit an ordinary saucer. Keep the blotting paper damp by adding a few drops of water each day, but do not allow water to lie in the saucer. Germination varies with the type of vegetable—anything between three to ten days. If the seeds are good, then most of them will germinate at the same time, but it is as well to leave them a further two days to allow late comers to make their appearance. If eight or more germinate out of ten, then the sample is good and you can expect good results. If less than five germinate, then it is as well to carry out a further test to make quite sure. In cases where the germination percentage is low, but the seeds have to be used as no others are available, sow them more thickly than is recommended.

STORAGE

Traditionally, seed is stored in laboratory desiccators, using either silica gel or calcium oxide as a desiccant. But seed stores quite well in wide-necked, screwtop jars containing a packet of silica gel crystals. These crystals absorb any moisture and allow the seeds to remain dry. The crystals should be taken out periodically and dried in the oven for three or four hours.

The length of time seeds can be stored and still give good germination varies with the type of vegetable. Tomatoes and beans will remain good for several months, while sweet pepper spoils after a few weeks. Lettuce seed absorbs moisture very easily and in the tropics needs very careful storage.

Weevils and boring insects constitute another danger, and it is advisable to mix D.D.T. dust with seeds before they are stored. Beans and peas are particularly susceptible.

PLANTING

Methods of planting will be found under each crop later in this book, but generally it can be said that large seeds are planted direct into beds and small seeds in boxes or baskets, the young seedlings being transplanted later into the beds. The small seeds are first planted into boxes so that they can get extra care and attention. It also means that beds are used to capacity for the longest possible period.

Locally-made baskets are ideal for this purpose as they have adequate drainage and are light to carry. Their one disadvantage is that if not moved carefully, soil will drop through the cracks.

If boxes are used, they should be shallow and made of light wood for ease in handling. There should be narrow gaps between the bottom boards to give drainage, large enough to allow for swelling when the wood gets damp.

A good mixture for seedboxes is 3 parts of top-soil, 2 parts of compost and 1 part of sharp river sand. The top-soil should contain as much fibrous root material as possible, and should be carefully examined for grubs and beetles before use. The compost should be mature and not hot. To each bushel (60 lbs.) of the mixture, add 1 lb. superphosphate, in order to stimulate root formation. Mix well together, fill the boxes and firm down gently with a piece of board. Take care not to firm down too much or the soil will consolidate. And (this cannot be stressed too much) do not overcrowd the seedboxes. The more thinly the seeds are planted, the more robust will be the plants, and of course they will be infinitely easier to transplant.

Place the seedboxes in partial shade, under trees, on a convenient verandah, or in a nursery shed like the one illustrated in Fig. 4. To keep the soil moist (not only the top but underneath as well) cover with board or cardboard. Remove the board each day to check on germination. As soon as the first seedlings emerge, remove the board completely or they will rot off.

The seedlings should not be too heavily shaded or they will reach out for the light and be weak in growth. There will also be a danger of 'damping off', which is discussed in the next chapter. Protect them from heavy rain as this will smash down young growth.

It is better to keep the seedboxes raised off the ground as this minimises the danger of insect attack. Spray also with the appropriate insecticide. Wood ash is a good deterrent to insects if sprinkled through the seedlings; it does not kill the pests, but they dislike it and will avoid areas so treated.

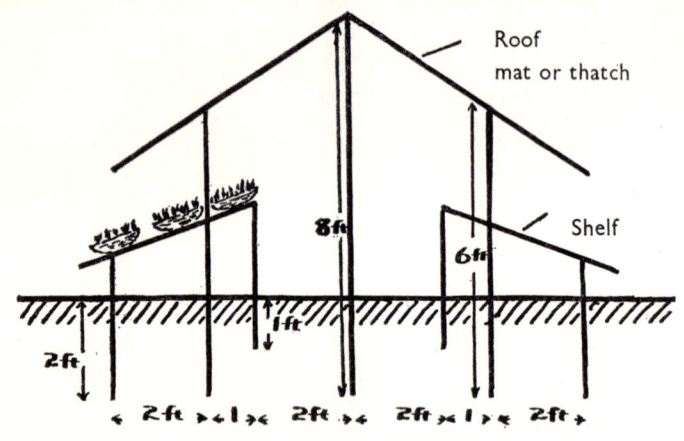

Fig. 4. Nursery shed

WATERING

This can only be decided on the spot. As a guide, push a finger into the soil to a depth of over one inch. If the soil feels moist at that depth, do not water. If it feels dry, water with a fine-rosed watering can, or even a cigarette tin. A cigarette tin with small holes punched in the base is a very useful little gadget for this kind of work.

Chapter 6 FIGHTING PESTS AND DISEASES

Each year more and more chemicals are being offered to gardeners for use against pests and diseases. In a book of this size it is only possible to deal with the more common of these compounds and indicate which of them should be used with care. At the same time, it is necessary to give a general warning against most of them, since they contain chemicals which not only kill insects and diseases but are also harmful to man and domestic animals. *Do be careful to read the instructions printed on containers, and keep them all out of the reach of children and animals.* Many of the newer mixtures contain more than one type of insecticide or fungicide and it is essential to read all instructions carefully. Use only the quantities recommended for a double strength application rarely doubles results and may instead do harm. At best, using more than is recommended is just a waste of money.

Do remember that all insects to be found in a garden are not harmful to plants. Examples are the pollinating insects such as bees, those which live on other insects such as the ladybird and praying mantis and, finally, those which are only a danger at a certain stage of their lives, such as butterflies and moths. These latter do no damage in the adult stage and often act as pollinating insects, but in the caterpillar stage they are a menace as they feed on foliage.

An insecticide is a chemical that kills insects. Its action may consist of poisoning the food eaten by the insect so that it dies from food poisoning. Such insecticides are known as 'Stomach Poisons'—lead arsenate is an example. They are extremely poisonous to man and are not now generally used as a spray on vegetables.

A second group of insecticides poisons the insect by entering its body through the pores. Yet a third group produces fumes which are absorbed by the insect in the same way and suffocates it. In addition, there are insecticides which combine the properties of the second and third groups.

Contact Poisons and Fumigants

Derris: A powder made from the root of the derris plant. The active part is called Rotenone and is used as a fish poison in many tropical countries. As it is not dangerous to man or animals, it can be used on vegetables right up to the time of harvest. Whether bought in dust form or for mixing with water, it must be applied to the insects themselves and not wasted on the foliage.

Pyrethrum: A powder made from the flowers of the pyrethrum. The active part is Pyrethrin. It is included in many insecticides because of its ability to 'knock down' the insect quickly, although the other parts of the insecticide may do the actual killing. This, too, can be used right up to harvest.

DDT: This is probably now universally known. It has a long-lasting effect, but does not cause immediate death. As a general rule, DDT should not be used later than within fourteen days of harvest, but the label on the container should be consulted for guidance. Do not use on cucumbers, squash or melons.

BHC: Sold under many trade names and in many different strengths. Is similar in action to DDT, but as it leaves a taint behind, it is as well not to use it so near harvest as DDT. Do not use on cucumbers, squash, melons, maize, beans, young tomato plants or tuber and root crops.

Lindane: A very valuable general insecticide, containing the pure gamma BHC. It is available in various strengths as a dust, wettable powder and liquid. Can be used on edible crops against caterpillars and aphids right up to harvest. Should not be used on maize, young cucumbers or tuber and root crops. In action, similar to BHC.

Malathion: Very toxic to a wide range of insects, but has low toxicity for man. Is very volatile, giving off its fumes quickly and killing the insects. Generally it should not be used within seven days of harvest, but again, consult the label.

Chlordane: Should only be used on edible crops when they are immature. It is effective against many types of caterpillar, beetle and grasshopper. Should not be used on cucumbers, squash and melons, unless stated otherwise on the label.

Diazinon: Can be used not only against aphids, mites, beetles, caterpillars and grasshoppers on the plants, but also as a soil fumigant against some soil pests. Should not be used within seven days of harvest.

Parathion: Highly toxic to humans and warm-blooded animals. *USE, ONLY AFTER VERY CAREFUL STUDY OF THE DIRECTIONS FOR USE ON THE LABEL.*

Fungicides

Fungus diseases represent one of the tropical gardener's main problems particularly in the more humid regions.

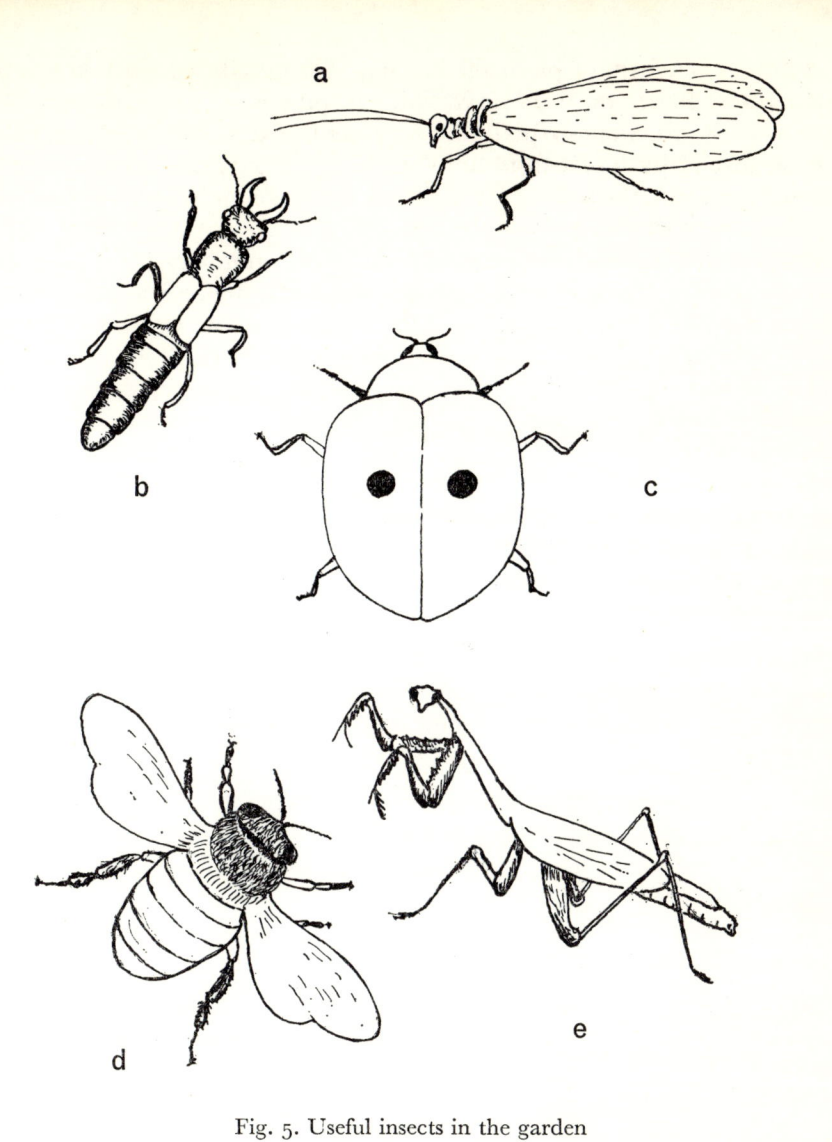

Fig. 5. Useful insects in the garden
(a) Lacewing (approx. 1 inch); (b) Rove Beetle (approx. ¾ inch); (c) Ladybird (approx. $\frac{1}{16}-\frac{1}{4}$ inch); (d) Bee; (e) Mantis (approx. 2–3 inches)

A fungus is a form of plant life lacking chlorophyll, which takes its food from other plants or dead material. A fungus is generally spread by 'spores' or germs, often so small that they can be carried by the wind. They can be spread by insects and animals, and the gardener himself can unwittingly spread them by getting them on his hands and clothes when working amongst infected plants.

Because the spores are produced in great numbers, fungus diseases spread rapidly. It is necessary not only to take immediate action when the disease is noticed, but to spray at intervals later to kill any fresh outbreak. In the seasons when humidity is high these diseases will be at their worst, and it is wiser to make a preventive spraying rather than wait for the diseases to appear. It is an old saying 'Prevention is better than cure', but how true in this case.

As with insecticides, there are now many fungicides offered by commercial firms, some of which are produced for particular diseases on certain crops. It is therefore important to read labels carefully, since a fungicide used on the wrong crop may damage or kill the plants. The more common fungicides are listed below.

Bordeaux Mixture: One of the oldest, and still considered one of the best of the general fungicides. It is made from copper sulphate and quicklime. Excellent for most crops, but should not be used on cucumbers, squash or young melons.

Lime-sulphur Solution: Stir 2 ozs. of freshly-slaked lime into 4 gallons of water. This is a fairly long process as the lime is difficult to dissolve. Then add gradually 1 oz. flowers of sulphur, stirring until dissolved. Strain before use.

This solution can be used on cucumbers, squash and melons against mildew. Do not store in a metal container.

Zineb: One of the newer fungicides derived from zinc and produced under various trade names. It can be used on most crops against blights and leaf spots. It is particularly successful on tomatoes, melons, cucumbers, onions, potatoes, peppers and lettuce.

Maneb: Similar in action to Zineb and can be used on the same crops.

Cheshunt Compound. Very useful for spraying the soil in seedboxes or in seed beds against 'damping-off' in the seedlings. The compound is made by mixing 2 ozs. powdered copper sulphate (Bluestone) with 11 ozs. powdered ammonium carbonate. Place in a glass jar or bottle for a day. Use 1 oz. of the mixture to 2 gallons of water and mix well before spraying.

SOIL FUMIGANTS

There are many troublesome pests in the soil which, if allowed to become too numerous, will cause considerable damage to roots. Probably the most

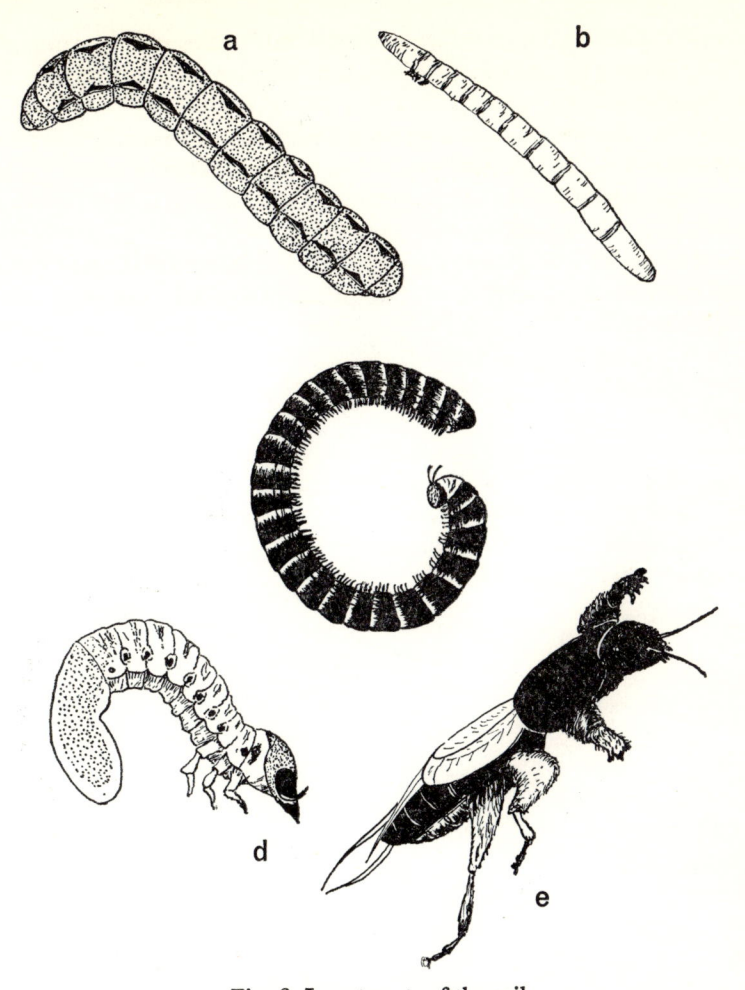

Fig. 6. Insect pests of the soil
(a) Cutworm (approx. 2–2½ inches); (b) Wireworm (approx. ½ inch); (c) Millipede (approx. 3 inches); (d) White Grub (approx. 1–1½ inches); (e) Mole Cricket (approx. 1 inch)

widespread is root knot eelworm, which multiplies at an amazing rate and can quickly ruin crops. Others are wireworms, millipedes and the larva of beetles.

These pests can only be destroyed by fumigating the soil. The easiest way is to inject a liquid fumigant along the vegetable beds. This will later turn into a lethal gas. Or a powder may be used. This gives similar results when acted upon by soil moisture.

There are many compounds available, including DDT and Nemagon, but they must be used with care, like other pesticides, and kept out of the way of children.

Chapter 7. HOW LOCATION, ALTITUDE AND RAINFALL WILL AFFECT THE VEGETABLES

We have noted in the foregoing chapters that vegetables have their likes and dislikes with regard to soil, and we have also seen how soils can to some extent be changed to meet these preferences. But the picture is not complete. There are three further factors we must study before we can start on our planting programme—geographical position, altitude and rainfall. Let us take each one separately and see how they affect us.

GEOGRAPHICAL POSITION

Even within the tropics, distance from the equator has a great bearing on what can or cannot be grown successfully, for whereas on the equator, the day length remains the same throughout the year, the father north or south we move, the day length changes as definite seasons emerge. It is this variation which affects growth. In the growth cycle of many root crops the period of shortening day length is the season when a reserve of food is formed in the root. Under the long-day conditions of the equator, the plant does not need to conserve this food. It grows well vegetatively and produces seed but, of course, no thickened root. Once we move north or south of the equator, where the day length changes with the emerging seasons, thicker roots are formed.

Day length does not affect root crops alone. Some types of beans and many varieties of onion which will not produce a crop near to the equator, prove increasingly successful the further north or south one goes.

ALTITUDE

Broadly speaking, altitude increases the range of vegetables that will give good yields. Garden eggs and peppers (happier at sea level) will give good yields at 2,000 feet. And at 5,000 feet, garden peas, potatoes and the large Savoy cabbage do extremely well.

RAINFALL

Two things here are important—the amount of rain and when it falls. In high rainfall areas where 80 inches or more is experienced over eight or nine months, leaf vegetables will thrive; tomatoes will grow (though some of the fruit may split after heavy storms); sweet potatoes do well. But most crops will need spraying, as fungus diseases are at their worst under these humid conditions.

Under a medium rainfall, well spread, it should be possible to grow good tomatoes, garden eggs, peppers, leaf and root vegetables.

Under drier conditions, melons will thrive and the deeper-rooted of the beans. Where watering is possible, some of the finest vegetables can be produced because of the absence of fungus diseases.

Full advantage should be taken of a marked dry season to plant at the middle to the end of the rains those vegetables which require good rains to support their first vegetative growth, and yet dry conditions for the ripening of the crop—onions are an excellent example.

And now we come to that aspect of tropical gardening which to my mind explains its fascination, for limitation of geographical position, altitude and rainfall, is not the whole of the story. These three combine to tell a very different tale. Let me choose three examples out of the many to illustrate what I mean.

On the equator, 2,000 feet with heavy rainfall: Here we can expect to grow good tomatoes for most of the year, as long as the main fruiting is not at the peak of the rains. A wide range of climbing beans through most of the year. Cucumbers and perhaps melons during the dry season. Irish potatoes and onions, a very good leaf lettuce and, possibly the Cos type as well, for most of the year.

10° North or South, 1,000 feet with medium rainfall: Most of the low altitude crops such as garden eggs, peppers and spinaches will do well. Tomatoes too, should yield good crops over most of the year. Leaf and head lettuce will grow, and also those varieties of cabbage best suited to the lower altitudes.

23° North or South, at sea level, with medium rainfall: Because of the distance from the equator, we could expect to grow most of those crops and their varieties designated for the highlands. Highland varieties of cauliflower, celery and cabbage. Lower altitude varieties will also do well, as will also Irish potatoes, most of the root vegetables, tomatoes (such as 'Manalucie'), garden eggs, sweet peppers, melons and pumpkins.

Possibilities are tremendous, but do remember that the varieties recommended in later chapters, whilst having considerable tolerance to tropical conditions, should not be tried outside the recommended altitude range unless distance from the equator cancels out lack of altitude.

II. BEANS, PEAS AND PULSES

The vegetables in this Section are all rich in protein, which is necessary for the building and maintenance of our body tissues. If eaten green (not dried) they provide a valuable source of vitamins B and C, which help to promote a healthy nervous system, assist the proper functioning of the digestion and maintain the blood in good condition. Unfortunately, not nearly enough beans are used in their green state and consequently the full benefits of the vitamins are largely lost.

There is such a wide range of beans and peas which can be grown in the tropics that, with correct planning of plantings and selection of the right type or variety for the season and location, it is possible to have a supply of fresh produce most of the year.

Chapter 1   FRENCH, SCARLET RUNNER AND LIMA BEANS

FRENCH BEANS: Phaseolus vulgaris (climbing): *P. vulgaris* var. *humulis* (bush or dwarf)

Common names: French, Kidney, Runner, Snap, String Beans.

Either in the dwarf or climbing form, this bean is probably the most widely grown in gardens throughout the tropics. It has a great tolerance to a wide range of conditions and can be grown successfully from sea level up to the highlands, and will do well if the rainfall is medium or above. Under high rainfall (over 60 inches a year) it is best to plant the climbing varieties during the main rains, as the pods of dwarf varieties often rot when in contact with wet soil or mulch. They can be grown successfully on most soils, from sandy to heavy clay, and although a slightly acid soil is to be preferred, anything in the range of pH 5·5 to 7·5 is acceptable.

Dwarf varieties will give good results if planted in the late rains. If well watered, plantings can be carried on into the dry season. The climbing varieties give the best results from plantings made at the early part of the rainy season.

SUITABLE VARIETIES	CLIMBING	DWARF
	Canadian Wonder	Kentucky Wonder
	The Prince	Tender and true
		Earliest of all

Double-dig the soil as French beans are deep-rooted and will benefit and then, if your soil is acid, give an application of lime. Fork it in to the top 3 inches of soil, and then leave the bed for a few days before applying compost or animal manure. Use well rotted compost or animal manure at the rate of at least 2 bushels (about 120 lbs.) for each 100 square feet of bed. At the same time scatter 1 lb. of a good mixed fertiliser over the same area. If the soil is sandy, this can be rasied to 2 lbs. If you have super-phosphate and sulphate or muriate of potash available, use $\frac{1}{2}$ lb. of each instead of the mixed fertiliser, and again double the quantity for poor, sandy soils. If you cannot get fertiliser locally, wood ash and crushed bones can be used, but twice the amount should be applied.

During the rainy season, the seeds of both climbing and dwarf varieties are best planted direct into the bed. In the dry season it is advisable to plant the seeds in boxes and transplant the seedlings into the beds when they are about 3 inches high. This will enable the young seedlings to have a little extra care, and the results will repay the extra work. Before planting, it is advisable to inspect the seeds. During storage, bean seeds are often attacked by weevils and boring insects, and any seeds with holes in or which are chipped should be discarded.

Do not plant the seeds at a greater depth than $1\frac{1}{2}$ to 2 inches. It does not matter whether they are planted lengthwise or upright, as they germinate just as well either way. With good fresh seed that has been well stored, plant one seed per hole. Germination should take place within a week of planting.

A 4-foot wide bed will take three rows of the dwarf and two rows of the climbing varieties. Space the seeds 9 inches apart in the rows, and then mulch the bed so that soil moisture is conserved. Remove the mulch when germination is seen, leaving a clear area of 3 inches radius around each seedling. This minimises the risk of attack by insects at a time when the stems of the seedlings are particularly tender. Where insect attack is likely to be serious, it is wise to place metal or bamboo collars around each plant immediately after germination. Metal containers are easily made by removing the tops and bottoms of small milk tins. For bamboo collars, use large bamboo and cut it into 3-inch pieces. These collars will stop insect attack and the plants grow quite happily in them, and they can be used over and over again.

Climbing varieties will have to be staked. As soon as germination is noticed, press in 6-foot stakes to a depth of $1\frac{1}{2}$ feet, deep enough to prevent them from being blown over when carrying the full weight of the vine when it is in full bearing. In order not to damage the roots, push them in no nearer than 2 inches from the seedlings.

Altitude and climate will, of course, affect the length of time before beans can be harvested, but as a guide you can expect to begin harvesting the dwarf varieties about 45 days after planting. The crops should continue for over a month. It takes a little longer to reach first harvest with climbing varieties—about 70 days. They too will continue for well over a month. When harvesting, do not leave the pods on the vine too long. They should be picked before the shape of the individual seeds can be seen for if left beyond this time the pods tend to become fibrous. The complete pod of all French beans is edible, although it is usual to remove a thin layer around the sides before slicing, as this part can be stringy.

SCARLET RUNNER   *Phaseolus coccineus*, syn. *P. multiflorus.*

Common names: Scarlet Runner, Multiflora bean.

This robust, climbing bean is essentially for the higher altitudes. At 5,000 feet and above it will give good yields. At lower altitudes, the flowers usually fail to set seed. It is tolerant to most soil types and can be grown under high rainfall very satisfactorily.

Follow the planting details already given for climbing French beans, except for planting distance in the rows.   The Scarlet Runner, as it is very robust, should be planted $2\frac{1}{2}$ feet apart in the rows, with 2 rows to a 4-foot wide bed.

First harvest can be expected above $2\frac{1}{2}$ months after planting, and will continue for at least three months.

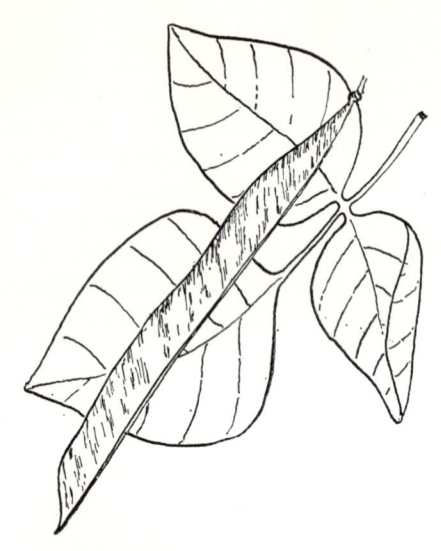

Fig. 7. Scarlet Runner Bean

LIMA BEANS   *Phaseolus lunatus*

Common names: Lima-, Sieva-, Tonga-, Rangoon-, Madagascar-, Java bean.

The Lima bean, either in its Bush (dwarf) or Pole (climbing) form is well known throughout the tropics, growing at its best at the lower altitudes and under medium to high rainfall.   It appears to be tolerant of a wide range of soils and can usually be grown successfully in locations which favour the growing of French beans.

Bush varieties produce good yields when planted during the early rains, while Pole varieties can be planted throughout the rains, later plantings maturing during the dry season.

SUITABLE VARIETIES   BUSH TYPE
                                              Burpees Bush
                                              Fordhook Bush
                                              Henderson's Bush

There are many local varieties of the Pole type which give satisfactory results.

Double-dig the beds. If the soil is very acid, apply lime. Follow in a few days with 2 bushels of compost or animal manure per 100 square feet forked into the top soil, and use $2\frac{1}{2}$ lbs. of mixed fertiliser for the same area. If you have stocks of separate fertilisers, use equal parts of superphosphate or muriate of potash at the same rate. If none is available, use crushed bones and wood ash in equal parts at double the above rate. Fertilisers are best applied ten days before planting the seed, to prevent damage through burning.

Plant the seeds direct into the bed at a spacing of 9 inches apart in the rows, with 3 rows to a 4-foot wide bed for the Bush varieties and 2 rows for the Pole varieties. As seeds rot fairly easily, do not plant deeper than 1 inch. If the seed is good, germination should take place within seven days. Stake the Pole varieties as soon as possible after germination.

Pole varieties planted at the end of the rains will need adequate supplies of water during the dry season; although they are deep-rooted, if allowed to dry out the crop will be very poor.

Harvesting of the Bush varieties usually begins about 45 days after planting and should continue for about two months, though this depends on weather conditions. The Pole varieties are slower to come into production, usually about $3\frac{1}{2}$ months, and will continue for a further $2\frac{1}{2}$ months. Pods should be picked as soon as the shape of the individual bean can be seen as if left longer, the seeds get tough. In some countries the pods are also eaten, but this may be only local varieties.

If the beans are to be stored, leave on the plant until the seeds rattle inside, and then inspect them for boring insects and grubs before putting them in screw-top jars.

In some local varieties the seed can be red, brown or spotted, and in these varieties when ripe, the seed coating contains sufficient prussic acid to be dangerous. As a general precaution, coloured seeds of these beans should be boiled twice to make sure that the acid has been discarded. The acid is present only when the beans are dried. In the green state there is no risk.

Unless this bean is a great favourite, one bed of the Pole type planted in the mid-rains and another towards the end of the rainy season, should be sufficient. A monthly planting of the Bush type during the rains should provide enough for a family of four.

Chapter 2 THE WINGED AND SWORD BEANS

WINGED BEAN *Psophocarpus tetragonolobus*

Common names: Winged-, Goa-, Asparagus-, Manilla-, Princess bean.

This vigorous climbing bean, a native of southern Asia, is well known in India and is now becoming better known in many parts of tropical Africa. The pods, which are often up to 14 inches in length, have frilled wings at each of the four corners. The seeds are round and brown.

It is essentially a bean for the low altitudes and humid conditions which prevail in most coastal districts. It thrives under high rainfall. It will grow well in sandy soils, but better yields will be obtained on richer types of soil. As it has a tuberous root, it will, however, continue to bear well in the dry season if it has established itself before the rains cease. Highest yields will be obtained from plantings made in the early rains. No commercial varieties of this bean are known.

Beds should be double-dug before planting, and receive 2 bushels of compost per 100 square feet, together with 2 lbs. of mixed fertiliser for the same area.

Do not plant deeper than 1 inch. and space 9 inches apart in the rows, with 2 rows to a 4-foot wide bed. Always keep the bed heavily mulched, but do not allow the mulch to come right up to the young plants. Stake as soon as possible, bearing in mind that this bean develops very heavy foliage which can easily be tossed about in a strong wind and damage the roots, with a resultant drop in yield or death of the plant.

The harvest of the young pods can begin within three months of planting, and continue for another 2 to 3 months. Do not allow the pods to get too large, for they are at their best if picked before the frilly wings become hard and fibrous.

Winged beans are an excellent substitute for French beans in the low lying humid areas. The pods are sliced sectionally, not lengthwise, and present an attractive star shape. This bean also provides edible foliage from the young shoots, an edible tuberous root and the beans when dried can be quite a delicacy when roasted.

One bed of Winged bean should provide sufficient for a family of four. If plantings are so arranged that one is made at the middle to the end of the rains, it will provide a valuable addition to the diet during part of the dry season.

SWORD BEAN *Canavalia ensiformis*

Common names: Sword-, Jack-, Horse bean.

This strong-growing, small climbing bean is particularly suited to difficult climates where most popular types may not flourish. The roots go very deep and the plant can therefore withstand very dry conditions, but on the other hand, it grows well under the heaviest rainfall. It is at its best only at the lower altitudes. Is not particular to soil type, often giving good results in sandy soils.

The best planting time is during the rains. The bean takes longer than most to bear pods and this enables it to be harvested in the dry season when other beans are perhaps in short supply.

Because of its deep roots, it responds to soil that has been double-dug. Applications of compost and fertiliser at the rates given for winged beans above, will increase yields.

Plant the large white seeds not more than 2 inches deep, with a 2-foot spacing between seeds in the row and $2\frac{1}{2}$ feet between the rows. Germination should be complete in about 7 days and is usually very high. No staking is necessary as the plants tend to be more bushy than climbing. The thick, leathery foliage, does not seem to be troubled by insects and special measures are rarely necessary.

Full-grown pods can be over a foot long and $1\frac{1}{2}$ inches wide, but if intended as a substitute for French bean, they should be gathered when only half grown when they are tender and easily sliced. If allowed to mature they are too fibrous for use as a green bean, but the large white bean can be extracted and stored. They can be used, boiled, but the skins should be

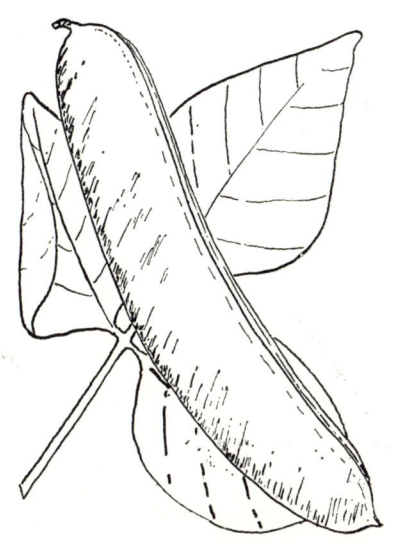

Fig. 8. Sword Bean

removed before consumption as they contain prussic acid; prussic acid is not present in the young green beans.

The first harvest can be taken at about 5 months and thereon, as the plant is a perennial, for as long as the plant lives. It is more usual, however, to treat the Sword bean as an annual and uproot when the main crop has been harvested, in about 9 to 10 months. The foliage makes good compost.

This bean should only be grown when a robust substitute for other better-quality bean types is needed. Usually one bed will be sufficient.

Chapter 3   COWPEAS AND GARDEN PEAS

COWPEA   Vigna sinensis

Common names: Cowpea, Tonkin-, Jerusalem-, Blackeye pea.

The cowpea is one of the most widely grown legumes in the tropics. It is used not only for human food, but also for cattle forage and green manuring. A multitude of varieties has been developed specifically for each of these purposes and therefore many of them will be of little use to the home gardener since they produce either dry peas or lush vegetation. Much work has been done in recent years in developing varieties with thicker fleshy pods, making them a valuable garden vegetable.

The cowpea grows more vigorously at the lower altitudes, but will grow up to 5,000 feet. Medium to high rainfall produce the highest yields. There does not appear to be a marked preference to any soil type and good results are obtained on poor sandy soils, if fertiliser is added.

Can be planted at most seasons, provided sufficient water is given during the dry season; yields will be highest from plantings made during the rains.

SUITABLE VARIETIES   DWARF
New Era
Bombay
Blackeye
Alabama

There are many good local varieties of the climbing type, but none seem to rank for commercial recognition.

The Cowpea, which is a true bean, is extremely useful in the garden as it is a host plant to nitrogen-fixing bacteria. These bacteria form nodules on the roots, and are capable of taking nitrogen from the air and transforming it into soluble nitrogen salts in the soil. The growing of this crop, for this reason, will greatly improve the soil, making it far richer in nitrogen salts after the crop has finished than when it was planted.

First double-dig the beds and then apply compost at the rate of 2 bushels per 100 square feet of bed, together with mixed fertiliser at 2 lbs. for the same area, all forked into the top-soil.

Seed of the dwarf varieties should be planted 9 inches apart in the rows, with 3 rows to a 4-foot wide bed. Plant no more than $1\frac{1}{2}$ inches deep and then mulch the bed with grass cuttings. When the young plants are 2 to

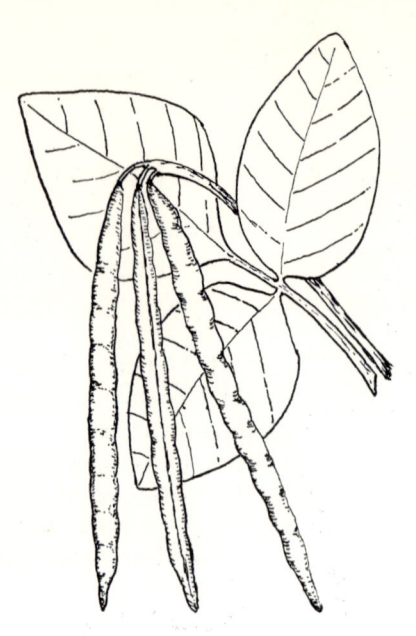

Fig. 9. Cowpea

3 inches high, remove the mulch from around them. Space climbing varieties 9 inches apart in the rows, with 2 rows to a bed.

The first green pods should be harvested as soon as the shape of the seeds can be clearly seen—between 2 and $2\frac{1}{2}$ months after planting, according to variety and conditions. Harvest of the dwarf varieties should continue for another month, and longer for the climbing varieties.

The green beans are used in the same way as French beans, but are usually sliced across and not lengthwise. Any surplus to requirements can be left to ripen fully on the plants until the seeds rattle inside, and these can then be shelled and stored, after inspection for weevils and borers.

If cowpeas are grown at the same time as French or other beans, limit plantings to one bed a month. This should be enough for a family of four.

THE CATJANG Vigna sinensis var. *cylindrica*

Is very like the Cowpea, but has slightly rounder pods. In all respects, the culture is the same.

ASPARAGUS BEAN Vigna sesquipedalis syn. *Dolichos sesquipedalis*

Common names: Asparagus bean, Yard-long bean.

This bean, a native of southern Asia, and now grown throughout the tropics, is much like the climbing Cowpea. The pods, however, are much longer—up to 3 feet, which prompts its common name. When green, they are slightly inflated, and are much more flabby than the Cowpea or French bean.

Does well at the lower altitudes and can flourish under high rainfall conditions; it should be grown in preference to dwarf Cowpeas in these areas.

Should be planted at the spacing given for climbing Cowpeas and during the rains. Harvesting should be over the same period as the Cowpea, but the yields will often be higher.

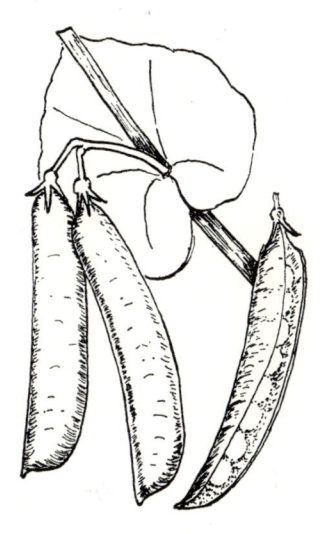

Fig. 10. Garden Pea

GARDEN PEA *Pisum Sativum*

Common names: Garden Pea, English Pea.

The Garden Pea has long been a favourite in colder climates, but its recent years with the wider distribution of canned and frozen foods, in popularity has spread throughout the world. It is probably not widely known that it has been grown successfully in the tropics, for it was considered only suitable for highland gardens, above 5,000 feet.

If the correct varieties are used, it is possible to grow this vegetable at any height above 500 feet, and even at sea level at the northern and southern limits of the tropics. Except at the higher altitudes, however, it is not an easy vegetable to grow and beginners should leave it until they have had a little more experience.

SUITABLE VARIETIES

Kelvedon Wonder	15 inches high, early, heavy cropper
Little Marvel	18 inches high, early, very good yields
Onward	30 inches high, later than the above
Alderman	5 feet, late maturing, suitable for higher altitudes.

At any altitude, it needs a good well drained soil. Best results are obtained if 2 trenches are made along the length of a 4-foot wide bed, 1 foot deep and the same width. Into the bottom of the trenches scatter 1 bushel of compost per 25 feet, together with 1 lb. of superphosphate, mixing the top soil in with these to fill up to within 2 inches of the top. Into the remaining shallow trench sow the seeds in 2 rows, 9 inches apart and not more than 1 inch deep. Cover the trenches with fine chicken wire or mosquito netting, laid across sticks; this will stop birds from nipping out the tops of the plants as they emerge from the soil, which will ruin the plant. Mulch between and around the trenches with grass cuttings to conserve soil moisture.

When the seedlings are about 3 inches high, give a top dressing of sulphate of ammonia, taking care not to burn the leaves. This gives a boost in growth. Water during dry spells when 4 gallons per 25 feet of trench given twice a week should be adequate.

Dwarf varieties do not need staking, but tall ones must be given support. Twiggy brushwood is excellent for this purpose as they will cling to it.

Early varieties can be harvested 9 to 10 weeks after planting, the main crop varieties after 12 weeks and the tall varieties after 14 weeks.

There is no doubt that it is an achievement to grow one's own Garden peas in the tropics. If you haven't done so yet, try a bed with one of the dwarf varieties and see what results you can get.

Chapter 4 OTHER INTERESTING BEANS AND PULSES

BONAVIST BEAN   *Dolichos lablab*

Common names: Bonavist bean, Papapa, Hyacinth bean.

A strong climbing bean resembling the Lima. It can be grown as a perennial, but is more usually treated as an annual. This bean, which originated in tropical Asia, is now fairly widely grown throughout the tropics, more especially at low altitudes. It appears to do best under medium rainfall and requires a rich soil for good yields. Plantings can be made during the rains or in the late dry season.

SUITABLE VARIETIES
Darkness (black seeded)
Daylight (white seeded)

Culture is the same as that for Pole Lima, but with a spacing of 2 feet in the rows as it is far more robust in growth.

Harvest should start about $3\frac{1}{2}$ months after planting and should continue for several months. Harvest the pods, which resemble those of the Lima bean, when the seed shape can be clearly seen. Only the seeds are used. If it is the intention to store, leave on the vine until the seeds rattle, then after inspection for insects, store in screw top jars.

This bean makes an excellent substitute for the Lima bean. If grown at the same time as other beans, one bed shoud be sufficient to provide a change in diet.

MUNG BEAN   *Phaseolus aureus*

Common names: Mung bean, Green Gram.

This erect, hairy bean is well known in India, China, The East Indies and Hawaii. The small cylindrical 3 inch pods contain small green seeds, and these are eaten as a vegetable. The main use of the seeds, however, is for the production of bean sprouts, a delicacy used in many Chinese and Oriental dishes.

The Mung bean prefers a low rainfall, and gives best yields at from sea level to about 3,000 feet. There are many good local varieties, few of which have commercial recognition.

They are best planted during the early rains, 9 inches apart in the rows and with 3 rows to a 4-foot wide bed.

If wanted for immediate use, they should be picked when mature but not fully ripe. If wanted for the production of bean sprouts, they should be allowed to ripen fully on the plant, then shelled and stored till required. For sprouting, the beans are spread in pans and covered with a damp cloth to keep them slightly damp. The sprouts appear in a few days and should be used at once, when they will not only be delicious but highly nutritious.

PIGEON PEA   *Cajanus indicus* syn. *C. cajan*

Common names: Pigeon pea, Cajan, Congo bean, Red Gram.

Well known throughout the tropics. It is often a farm crop, but many farmers have a small plot in the compound to provide earlier and better seeds for the house. On the farms it is treated as a perennial, but in gardens it is grown usually as an annual.

Fig. 11. Pigeon Pea

It produces good yields under heavy rainfall of up to 90 inches a year, but it also thrives under low rainfall where other pulses will not produce good yields. It is very tolerant of a wide range of soil type, from limestone to acid, but naturally best yields will come from a rich soil.

Plantings can be made from the early rains to well into the rainy season. If grown as an annual, and this will be more general in gardens, plant the seeds 2 feet apart in the rows with 2 rows in a 4-foot wide bed, not more than 2 inches deep. Fertiliser can be given either before planting, as is the case with most beans and peas, or as a top dressing scattered between the plants when they are about 6 inches high. A good mixed fertiliser is suitable, using 2 lbs. for every 100 square feet of bed.

The first green pods should be ready to harvest in 5 to 6 months, and will continue in bearing for some months. The green seeds, although much smaller than the lima bean, are used in the same manner.

If you do decide to let some of the bushes grow on for another season, it is advisable to remove alternate plants so as to leave more room for those remaining. Cut them back after harvest and give another top dressing of mixed fertiliser.

In some countries the dried 'peas' are used for the production of bean sprouts, as has already been described under Mung bean.

SOY BEAN *Glycine Max* syn. *G. soja: G. hispida*

Common names: Soy bean, Soya bean.

This is another bean grown almost universally throughout the tropics. It originated in south-eastern Asia, where it is known to have been cultivated for some 4,000 years. In many parts, it is the most valuable source of vegetable protein and oil.

The Soy bean prefers the cooler climate of the higher altitudes up to 5,000 feet. Some varieties, however, in particular the yellow-seeded one, will grow well from 5,000 feet upwards. Rainfall must be well distributed; most varieties prefer not more than 50 inches a year. To produce good yields it needs a rich soil.

Usually plantings are made at the end of the rains, spaced 12 inches in the rows, with 2 rows to a 4-foot wide bed.

There are more than a thousand known varieties, but many of them are unsuitable for the production of green seeds for kitchen use, so it is advisable to use either Benares, Malayan or Bansei. If good varieties are known locally, these can of course be used.

Double-dig the beds and give an application of compost or animal manure at the rate of 2 bushels per 100 square feet, forked in, and then cover the bed with mulch. Germination is usually good, and the young plants will appear within a week of planting. It should be possible to harvest the green pods about 3 months after planting; they should be allowed to swell, but be picked before the colour starts to change. Only the green seeds are eaten. In some countries the dried seeds are used for bean sprouts, but are not considered to be as good as the Mung bean.

CLUSTER BEAN *Cyamopsis psoralioides*

Common name: Cluster bean.

This small perennial bush, growing to a height of 4 feet, derives its common name from the small hairy pods which grow in clusters at the

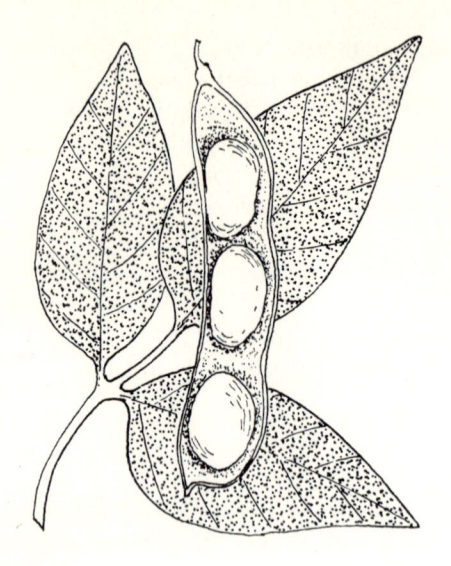

Fig. 12. Soy Bean

leaf axils. The seeds are white, black or grey, and are used either when young or in the dried state.

Grows best at the lower altitudes under medium rainfall; is not particular to soil, but of course gives better results if the soil is well drained and enriched with compost.

The planting suggestions given for the Soy bean can be applied here, but as the Cluster bean is a perennial, an application of fertiliser every six months, using 2 lbs. per 100 square feet, will increase yields.

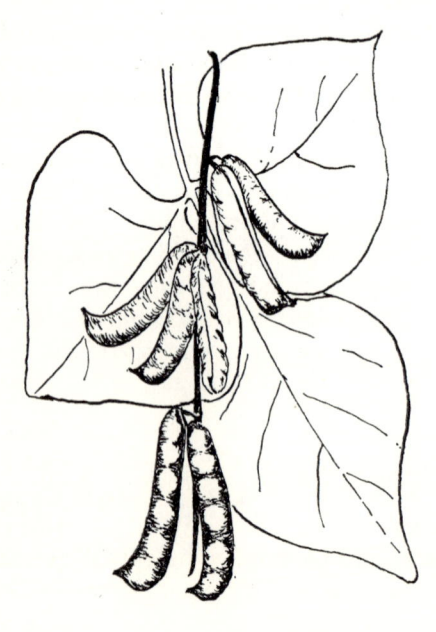

Fig. 13. Cluster Bean

GROUND NUT *Arachis hypogaea*

Common names: Groundnut, Peanut, Goober.

The groundnut is a very popular item of diet throughout the tropics. It can be eaten raw, roasted, used as peanut butter, or in rich stews. The oil processed from the nut is well known and it can be used for a salad oil as well as for cooking. Its food value is very high, and weight for weight, contains three times as many calories as beef. The Groundnut originally came from Brazil

The Groundnut is botanically of great interest as, when the flowers are fertilised, the ovaries are pressed down into the soil by the elongation of the flower stalk. It is after the ovaries reach the soil that the nuts are formed.

Grows best at the lower altitudes, from sea level to 3,000 feet, and prefers a sandy soil that has been enriched by fertiliser. Plant at the beginning of the rains.

During the last few years many new varieties have been developed, some giving far higher yields than the older ones. There are also varieties now that are resistant to the Rosette virus disease. Of the older varieties, 'Castle Cary' is considered very reliable.

If yours is not a sandy soil, it is advisable to double-dig to improve drainage. Extract the seeds from the shell and plant 3 to each hole at a spacing of 9 inches in the rows, with 4 rows to a 4-foot wide bed. Only extract seeds when required, as they store better in the shell.

When the seedlings are about 2 inches high, remove all the smallest and leave only one plant per hole. A dressing of superphosphate given a month after planting, scattering it around the plants, usually increases yields.

The nuts can be lifted from 4 to 5 months after planting. In harvesting, be sure that all are taken from the soil, or you will have a second crop coming up amongst the next crop. This may not appear a bad thing, but it must be remembered that all the spacings given for vegetables are given on the assumption that those vegetables will not have to compete with other plants. If there is competition from self-sown seedlings, there may not be enough plant food available for the whole of the crop and yields will probably be lower.

BAMBARRA GROUNDNUT *Voandzeia subterranea*

Common names: Bambarra or Madagascar Groundnut.

This is an ideal nut for very poor soils having a pH of 3.5 to 5.5, under medium rainfall and at low altitudes. It is used in the same way as the more well-known Groundnut, but is generally not considered as good.

Seeds should be planted at the beginning of the rains at the same spacing as that given for Groundnuts. Often gives as good yields as Groundnuts, especially on the poorer soils. The nuts are used in the same way as Groundnuts.

Chapter 5   PESTS AND DISEASES OF THE CROPS

COMMON PESTS

Unfortunately, these crops are subject to attack from a wide variety of insect pests, and it is important that the gardener should be able to identify them so that the correct chemical can be used immediately. And it must also be understood that a chemical which may be correctly used against a particular pest on, say, cabbage, may not be the right one to use on that same pest when it appears on beans.

Nematodes or eelworms are a serious threat to all the crops in this section. They live on the roots of beans and peas, and for that matter, many other vegetables, causing cyst-like swellings. The eelworm, living inside these swellings, extracts food from the roots, thus starving the plant and decreasing yield. They can multiply at an alarming rate and, if left unchecked, become a grave threat to a garden.

When clearing a bed of beans or peas, take them up carefully and examine the roots. If there should be masses of small boil-like eruptions on them, cut the roots off and burn them. It is important to take the plants up carefully with a fork, not merely pull them up. If merely pulled out of the ground the likelihood is that most of the eelworms will have been left behind ready to multiply and attack the next crop in greater number.

If, on inspection of the roots of your crop, you consider the eelworm population is getting too high, then the beds will have to be treated with a soil fumigant, which is quite a costly business. A compound such as Nemagon should be used.

It has been found that the use of large quantities of compost will help to depress an eelworm population as will also a correct rotation of crops. This rotation breaks up the breeding cycle. Corn is particularly useful as it will not act as a host plant to the eelworm.

Caterpillars attack leaves and sometimes pods. They vary greatly in size and colour, but most will succumb to a dusting of the plants and mulch with either DDT or Chlordane dust. Do not use Chlordane on plants which have started to form pods.

Bean Beetles are $\frac{1}{4}''$ or less in length and can be brown, red or black in colour. Some, like the Mexican Bean beetle, are spotted. They can all do considerable damage by chewing foliage.   Watch for signs of chewing on the younger leaves, as these are usually the first to be attacked.   Dust foliage and mulch with either DDT or Chlordane dust, but again, do not use the latter when the plants have started to form pods.

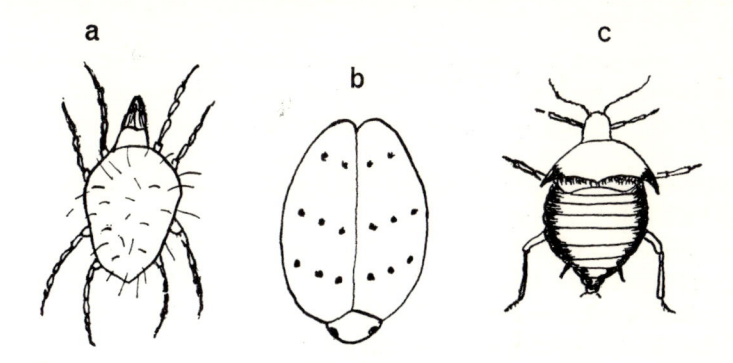

Fig. 14. Three Pests of Beans
(*a*) Red Spider Mite (approx. 1/60 inch); (*b*) Mexican Bean Beetle (approx. ¼ inch); (*c*) Aphid Nymph (approx. 1/10 inch)

Mites are the smallest of the pests and therefore easily overlooked. Probably the most widely distributed is the Red Spider mite. It will be found in colonies on the upper surface of leaves and at first glance looks like red pepper dust. The area of 'dust' is small to begin with, but enlarges rapidly as the mites multiply. The mites obtain food by sucking the leaves, damaging the leaf tissue which then starts to turn yellow and brown. A serious infestation can depress the yield considerably and leaves will drop off. Keep a watch for this pest in the dry season. As soon as it is observed, dust the plants with flowers of sulphur or Derris, or spray with wettable sulphur.

Aphids are usually most troublesome in the early rains. They are very small insects, only about 1/10th of an inch long, can be white or green, but more usually black, and are found in clusters usually on younger shoots. These suck the foliage and the area around dies through the damage. They depress yields. They also multiply at an alarming rate as the female can produce 300 young in a day. Derris is one of the best insecticides to use against them, as it can be used without danger to humans.

Serpentine Leaf Miner can effect cowpeas and sometimes certain of the beans. The grub lives between the upper and lower surfaces of the leaf and, as it chews its way along the leaves, leaves a pale track which may twist and turn. Not an easy pest to deal with. Diazinon can be used for spraying, but its use must be stopped at least seven days before harvest commences.

COMMON DISEASES OF BEANS AND PEAS

Virus diseases. These are diseases in the tissues of the plant and nothing can be done to cure them. Prevention is the only method of attack. Always buy good seed. The plants from which good commercial seed is taken have usually been inspected to make sure that they are free from these diseases.

As virus diseases are often transferred from one plant to another by piercing insects, such as aphids, any wild plants in the garden or neighbouring land showing symptoms of virus disease should be uprooted and burnt.

Two virus diseases attack the crops of this section—Rosette in groundnuts and Mosaic on Lima beans.

A groundnut plant attacked will be stunted and grow in the form of a rosette. The disease lowers yields considerably and can be spread from plant to plant until the whole bed is infected. There is no cure and affected plants should be uprooted and burnt. If the disease is known to be present in your locality, try to plant only varieties known to be resistant. If no such varieties are available, try planting at half the given distance, for this doubling of the number of plants seems to minimise the danger.

Affected Lima bean plants develop yellowish patches, clearly defined by the veins. Older leaves are usually affected first and then the symptoms gradually spread to younger growth. Again, there is no cure and affected plants should be uprooted and burnt.

Fungus diseases: These diseases are at their worst when night mist is followed by hot, sunny days. These conditions provide the ideal humidity and temperature for fungus spores to germinate when they alight on suitable plants. Generally, the more highly developed types of beans or peas, such as French beans, Lima beans and Garden peas, are most seriously affected. Those which have their origin in the tropics have more resistance. Five types of this disease may be encountered, and all are easily recognisable.

Anthracnose, which may affect French beans, can be recognised by small brown specks developing on the green pods; these will later develop into larger and darker sunken areas. The disease may penetrate to the seeds, which will develop yellow-brown spots and make them unusable. On no account should seeds having such spots be stored or used as seed, as the disease can be seed borne, which underlines the need for good quality guaranteed seeds. The spots may also develop on the leaves.

In its early stages, this disease can be controlled by spraying with Bordeaux Mixture when the foliage is dry.

Powdery Mildew mainly affects French beans, Cowpeas and Garden peas. It appears as a fine, white powdery coating on the upper leaf surfaces and can be easily overlooked at first when the powdery dots are widely separated. Later, the spots become more dense and increase until the whole plant is covered. A severe attack will ruin a crop, and even a mild attack will diminish yields.

As soon as the disease makes its appearance, the plants should be dusted with Flowers of Sulphur or sprayed with a sulphur-based or Maneb fungicide.

Downy Mildew is easily distinguishable from the above. It is found mainly on Lima beans, appearing first on the pods in the form of small, downy patches, quite unlike the minute powder spots of Powdery Mildew. The disease starts on the pods and then spreads to the leaves and stem. It will rapidly destroy a plant if not treated quickly.

Control by spraying with Zineb as soon as the first blossoms appear, and then at 7 to 10-day intervals. Bordeaux Mixture can also be used, but it is not so effective.

Bean Rust is usually worst on French Climbing beans, and appears in the form of red, powdery spots on the undersides of the leaves. When the attack is severe the leaves fall off. This disease can be spread by wind and, in rainy weather by the gardener himself, when spores are carried from one plant to another on tools or the hands of the gardener. It can be controlled by dusting with Flowers of Sulphur or spraying with a sulphur-based or Maneb-based fungicide.

Damping-off of seedlings: Here young seedlings bend over just above ground level and die. Close inspection will show that the stem has rotted. If you have had this trouble, then it is best to treat all seeds before planting with Spergon or Delsan, using it at the rate of 1 teaspoonful to 3 lbs. of seed. Thoroughly mix chemical and seed together in a closed container to make sure that all the seed is uniformly coated.

If you cannot get either Spergon or Delsan, spray the soil with Cheshunt Compound (see page 32).

III. TOMATOES, GARDEN EGG, PEPPERS AND GOURDS

In this Section will be found some of those vegetables which produce the delicious fruits so often highly priced in the market. A much greater variety of these could be grown, even under difficult conditions, with the use of the correct varieties, and also the use of the right chemicals to combat the pests and diseases to which they are prone.

Some of the fruits are of the highest dietetic value—the tomato and sweet peppers are outstanding examples—whilst others, such as cucumber and melon, with less food value, are still delicious and highly appreciated. Their food value is enhanced by the fact that many of them can be eaten in their raw state, which means that vitamins need not be lost in cooking.

Chapter 1   TOMATOES

THE RED TOMATO   *Lycopersicon esculentum*

Common names: Red Tomato, Love Apple, Tomati, Kamako.

The tomato originated on the slopes of the Andes in southern America and, according to some authorities, was brought to Great Britain in 1596. It was not until the present century, however, that it became popular as a food, and it is now grown universally.

The fresh fruits are rich in vitamins A, B and C. They can be grown from sea level up to at least 7,000 feet, and will tolerate a rainfall of up to 90 inches a year, though best results are obtained where there is a well distributed rainfall of from 30 to 50 inches a year, with a relatively low humidity. As a rich, deep soil is essential, beds should be enriched with compost and fertilisers to ensure that sufficient plant foods are available to the plant.

In areas of high rainfall, plantings are usually confined to the period from the middle of the dry season through to the middle of the rains. In medium or low rainfall areas, plantings can often be made throughout the year if facilities for watering are available; otherwise, plantings should be confined to the rainy season.

SUITABLE VARIETIES

The gardener has several hundreds of varieties from which to choose, but many of them are unsuitable for tropical conditions since they were originally developed for growing in the temperate regions. The varieties listed below have been tested under tropical conditions and have all given good yields of quality fruit. Both Dwarf and Tall types are given, and the differences between them should be studied first before making a selection.

The Dwarf or Bush tomato grows as a small bush and has the attraction that its sideshoots need not be removed. It is generally considered easier to grow and is therefore particularly useful to the beginner. In high rainfall areas a good crop can be set before the plants become seriously affected by fungus diseases—a very important factor where plantings are made during the main rains.

Fruit is produced near the ground and can be lost through rotting if it comes in contact with wet mulch. This danger is much more serious in high rainfall areas, and here it is essential to tie the fruit trusses to a stake.

Varieties of the Dwarf type produce their crop over a shorter period than those of the Tall type and this must be watched if surplus fruit is to be avoided.

Varieties of the Tall type will continue growing upwards (as long as they are provided with sufficient nutrients) until they are 7 to 8 feet high. Fruits will be borne up the length of the stem, but usually after the fourth truss the number and size of the fruits gets smaller. For this reason, it is usual to prevent the plant from producing more than four trusses by removing the growing point. This does not arise with the Dwarf type.

In both Dwarf and Tall types, different varieties vary considerably in size, colour and flavour. Those of American origin generally have larger and sweeter fruits, whilst those developed in Great Britain produce medium-sized fruits often sharper in taste.

	DWARF VARIETIES	TALL VARIETIES
BELOW 3,000 FEET	Dwarf Gem	Moneymaker
	Fargo's Bush	Harbinger
	Manalucie*	Prolific
		Manapal*
ABOVE 3,000 FEET	Fargo's Bush	Bonny Best*
		Marglobe*

Denotes varieties of American origin

To get the best results, tomato seeds should be planted in seedboxes or baskets, later transplanting the young plants into the vegetable beds. Soil mixture for the boxes or baskets has already been discussed on page 27. Plant the seeds individually 2 inches apart each way, and not more than $\frac{1}{4}$ of an inch deep. Cover with fine soil and water, either with a fine-rose watering can or a cigarette tin with small holes punched in the base. It is important to give this spacing of 2 inches apart as this enables the young plants to be removed later without damage to the roots. It is common practice to plant tomato seeds thickly in rows, but on transplanting this always means a severe check to the young plants because the roots are damaged when the seedlings are separated one from the other.

Cover the basket with a board or cardboard to exclude light and conserve soil moisture. From the fourth day on remove the board to check on germination. When germination has taken place, remove the board completely or the dark moist atmosphere will cause the seedlings to 'damp-off' and die.

To water, test with your finger to a depth of $\frac{1}{2}$ an inch below the surface. If dry at this depth, then it is safe to water. Too heavy watering produces thin, spindly plants, prone to disease. Too much shade also has this effect.

When the seedlings are about 4 inches high they are ready to be transplanted into the beds, which must be prepared well in advance to give the soil time to settle down.

Prepare the beds by digging two trenches the length of the bed, 9 inches wide and the same depth. Into the bottom scatter at least 1 bushel of compost or animal manure for every 25 feet. At the same time, sprinkle wood-ash or 1 lb. of muriate of potash along the trenches. Replace the soil and mulch the bed. Allow a week for the soil to settle.

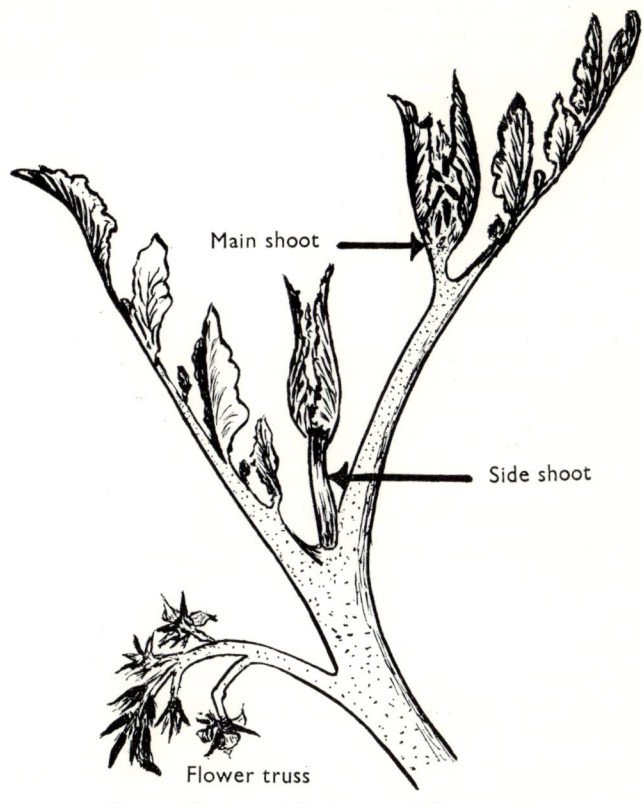

Fig. 15. Tomato side shoot and flower truss

Seedlings are best transplanted on a dull day or in the evening, when there is less chance of them wilting. An hour before removing the seedlings, water the seedbox well, as this helps to bind the soil to the roots. Take out separately, digging the fingers into the soil an inch from the plant and removing as much soil as possible adhering to the roots. Transplant at a distance of 18 inches in the rows, immediately along the line where the compost had previously been buried. Plant them at least an inch deeper than they were growing in the seedbox. The tomato, unlike most plants, will develop roots from the part of the stem now covered with soil. These roots are of great value to the plant later on as they enable it to take up additional food from the soil when this is needed later on to support a heavy crop of fruit.

After planting, make sure that the mulch does not come within 3 inches of the stem, for this can encourage insect attack. Well water the plants immediately and, if the weather is hot and dry, build up a little grass over each plant to prevent it wilting. Once the plants have become established in their new conditions, the grass can be removed.

After the initial watering, unless it is a particularly dry time, do not give any more for several days. This encourages the plant to make good root growth, for the roots will search for water. A few days after planting, test the soil. If it feels damp 2 or 3 inches down, do not water, but when you do water, give enough. A gallon a plant, given from a bucket held down close to the mulch, is a reasonable amount at a time. A sprinkling of water does more harm than good.

Most varieties are the better for staking, so that no fruit rests on the mulch, either to rot or be attacked by insects. But tall varieties must be staked, strong enough to carry the weight of the plant in full bearing and about 5 feet long. If the stakes are put in immediately after transplanting the seedlings, there need be no interference or damage to the root system. Push them in about 2 inches from the plant to a depth of 12 to 15 inches.

Tie the plant loosely to the stake with raffia, passing under the leaf joint, as shown in the illustration. The Tall varieties need tying every 9 inches, but with the Dwarf varieties only each branch need be supported.

As the plants develop, side shoots will be produced from the leaf axils. In the Dwarf varieties these should be left undisturbed, but they must be removed from the Tall varieties. When taking them out, do not mistakenly remove the growing point. This is easily done, so do study the diagram on page 61.

When the second truss of flowers begins to open, the plants will need more food. They should be given a top dressing of fertiliser, or later trusses will be very small. Use a good mixed fertiliser high in phosphate (P) and potash (K), at the rate of at least half a matchboxful a plant. First remove the mulch and then scatter round the plant in a ring—see the illustration on page 85. Replace the mulch. It is much better to give a top dressing like this every month than one big application. In the case of one large application, much of the benefit is lost because the plant cannot absorb it all quickly and that which is surplus to immediate requirements will be drawn down below the reach of the roots into the sub-soil.

Harvest from Dwarf varieties usually starts about 3 months after planting and the bulk of the crop should be ready in the succeeding 6 weeks. The Tall varieties take a little longer to come into bearing, but on the other hand harvest will continue for 3 to 4 months, according to season.

From plantings made during the rains, two beds should give enough fruit for a family of four, but if the fruit is required throughout the year, then it is better to make a planting of one bed every month throughout the season.

THE CURRANT TOMATO *Lycopersicon pimpinellifolium*

This tomato originally came from Peru, but it is now fairly widely grown as the fruits, which are only about $\frac{1}{2}$ an inch in diameter, are sweet and delicious when served whole in salads. A single truss may bear up to 25 fruits. They are well worth growing as they are easy and resistant to some of the fungus diseases.

Treat the plants as you would Dwarf tomatoes, but there is no need to stake them as long as the trusses are propped up off the ground.

Chapter 2 GARDEN EGGS AND PEPPERS

GARDEN EGG Solanum melongena var. esculentum.

Common names: Garden Egg, Egg Plant, Melongene, Aubergine, Brinjal.

Originally from southern Asia, most of the commercial varieties now grown were developed in America and Ceylon. The Garden Egg is now widely grown, not only in the tropics but also in the sub-tropical zones, and in the shape and colour of the fruits there is a wide range. The fruits of the recognised commercial varieties are usually far bigger than those obtained from local selections, and black or dark purple seem to be the favourite colours. There are, however, selections having fruits in white or yellow, violet, purple or black.

The Garden Egg thrives at the lower altitudes, from sea level to 1,000 feet, but it can be grown as high as 6,000 feet. At the higher levels, however, the plant is smaller and the yields are lower. It prefers medium to heavy rainfall, but can be grown in drier areas if watered well. To get the best yields, a deep, well drained soil is desirable, with additions of compost and fertiliser.

Plantings are usually confined to the rainy season, unless adequate water is available. In that case plantings may be attempted from the middle to the end of the dry season, but usually plants will be smaller and yields lower.

SUITABLE VARIETIES

Black Beauty	—	large round purplish-black fruit
Florida Market	—	long oval purplish-black fruit
Peradeniya (Ceylon)	—	long oval violet fruit
Florida High Bush	—	thick oval, purplish-black fruit

The seeds should be planted in seedboxes as already described on page 60 for tomatoes. Beds should be double-dug and receive compost at the rate of 2 bushels per 100 square feet and mixed fertiliser at 1 lb. for the same area, forked into the top soil.

Transplant the seedlings into the bed 2 feet apart in the rows, with 2 rows to a 4-foot wide bed. Mulching is essential as the plants wilt very easily in dry weather; this can be largely avoided if soil moisture is retained with a thick mulch.

It is not essential to stake the plants, but is a useful precaution against wind damage. In strong winds the plants can be blown about, branches ripped off and root systems ruined if the plant is blown over. If staking, 3-foot stakes should be sufficient.

When the first flowers appear, an application of a good mixed fertiliser helps to increase yields. Apply a matchboxful per plant in a ring round it, as already described for tomatoes. A similar dressing can be given each month.

The first fruits should be ready to pick about $2\frac{1}{2}$ months after transplanting and should continue for a further 4 months. These times will vary with season and variety. It is best to pick the fruits when they are half to three-quarters mature as the flavour is far superior to those left to mature completely, when the skin will also be tough.

Unless the Garden Egg is a strong favourite, one bed should be sufficient, as this will continue to crop throughout what will in most cases be the only season when they grow well.

BIRD PEPPER   *Capsicum annuum*

Common names: Bird-, Bird's eye-, Hot peppers.

This type of pepper is grown throughout the tropics—an essential item in all 'hot' soups and stews. It thrives at the lower altitudes and prefers medium rainfall. It can be grown on all types of soil.

All pepper seed lose their viability very quickly and, unless stored in sealed containers or a desiccator, will give poor results if more than three months old.

Plantings are usually made towards the end of the dry season, but can be made earlier than this if well watered.

The seed should go into seedboxes or baskets in the usual seed mixture, transplanting the seedlings into the beds when they are 3 to 4 inches high. Beds should be double-dug, limed if the soil is very acid, and then given an application of compost or animal manure at the rate of 2 bushels per 100 square feet with a dressing of mixed fertiliser at 1 lb. for the same area, both forked into the top soil. A 4-foot wide bed will accommodate 3 rows of seedlings, with an 18 inch spacing between the plants.

The first peppers should be ready to harvest about 3 months after planting; and at this time the plants will benefit from a top dressing of mixed fertiliser, using half a matchboxful per plant, given in a ring 6 inches from the stem. Harvest of the peppers should continue for several months.

If some of the fruits are to be stored, then they should be left to become fully red-ripe on the plant, and then laid out thinly in the sun. Take them in each night and put out each day when the sun is hot. The quicker they are dried, the better they will keep and the more pungent will be the flavour. Ground dried peppers are used a great deal in sauces.

Only the gardener can decide how much hot pepper he wants to grow—one family might be able to use the produce of 2 beds whilst another would find produce from half a bed more than enough.

CHERRY PEPPER   *Capsicum annuum* var. *cerasiforme*

The fruits of this type are cherry-shaped, about $\frac{1}{2}$ to 1 inch in diameter, and may be red, yellow or purplish. They are pungent and can be used in the same way as the Bird pepper. To grow, follow suggestions made above with regard to Bird pepper.

CAYENNE PEPPER   *Capsicum annuum* var. *longum*

Common names: Cayenne, Long-, Chilli-, Long Red-, Long Yellow Pepper.

The fruits are much longer than the two previous varieties, varying from 3 to 12 inches according to variety. All are thin, tapering and pungent. From them is obtained the Cayenne pepper of commerce.

Follow the same growing methods as given for Bird pepper. The first peppers should be ready for harvest in about 70 days and go on for several months.

SWEET PEPPER   *Capsicum annuum* var. *grossum*

Common names: Sweet Pepper, Bell Pepper, Pimento.

The fruits of the Sweet pepper are much larger than any of the varieties previously mentioned and can go up to 3 inches in diameter and 5 inches in length. They are hollow, thick walled, usually green when immature, turning red or yellow when ripe. Nutritious and delicious, the Sweet pepper is well known to most good cooks in hors d'oeuvres, salads, soups and stews, and stuffed and baked.

It can be grown successfully up to 6,000 feet, but usually does best between 500 and 1,000 feet. Main plantings are usually confined to the rainy season, but very good crops can be obtained from plantings made during the dry season if the plants are well watered and mulched. They grow well on clay soils if the drainage is good, and on sandy soils if they have been enriched with compost and fertiliser. Soil moisture is very important to this crop, and if it fluctuates a lot, due to heavy rain or poor drainage, the crop will be poor.

SUITABLE VARIETIES

'World Beater' and 'Californian Wonder' are both large-fruited, high-yielding varieties. Normally harvested when the fruits are still green, but they can be allowed to ripen to deep red.

'Neopolitan' and 'Cuban'. Fruits are not as thick as those previously named, are pale greenish-yellow when immature and red when ripe.

Prepare the beds by double-digging to ensure the best possible drainage. Give acid soils a dressing of lime, 1 to 2 lbs. will be enough for 100 square feet of a sandy soil, but rather more for a heavier clay type. If lime is applied, leave for a few days before adding compost or animal manure, at least 2 bushels for the same area. Mixed fertiliser can be applied at the same time, using at least 1 lb., and more on sandy soils. If fertiliser is not available, use at least 2 lbs. of wood ash for the same area. Fork all into the top soil and then mulch the bed heavily.

Stronger seedlings will be obtained if the seed is first sown in boxes or baskets, 2 inches apart each way. This spacing allows the young seedlings to be removed without damage to the roots. Use the seed mixture suggested on page 27.

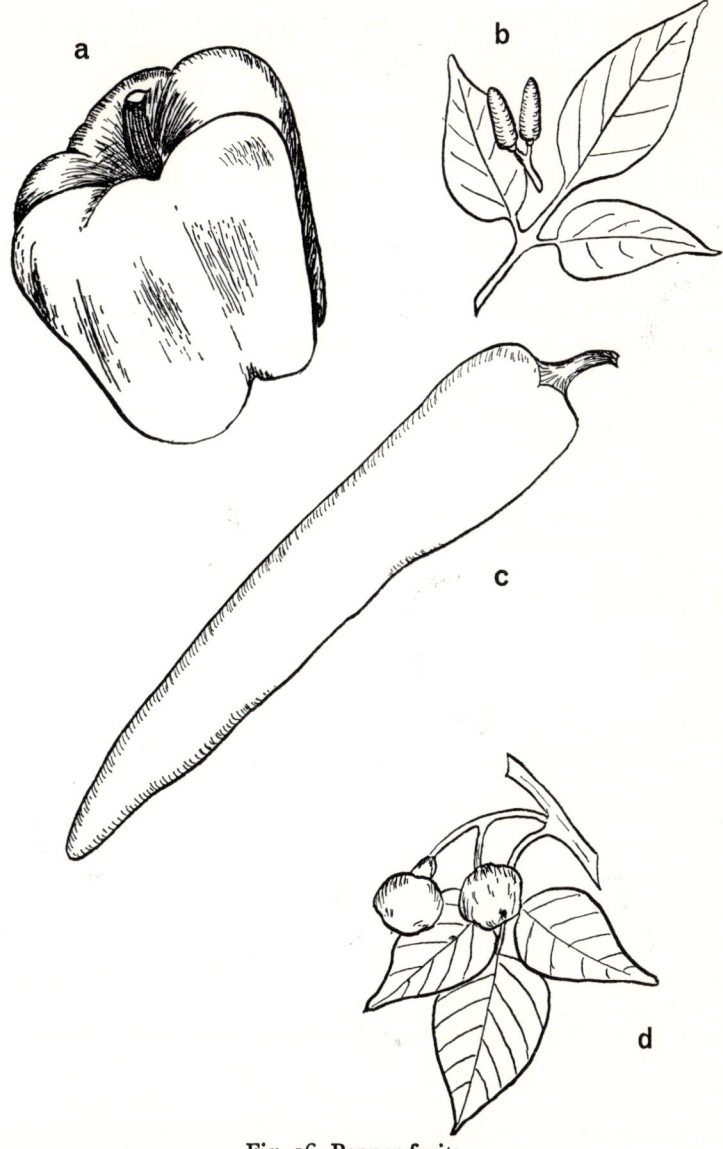

Fig. 16. Pepper fruits
(*a*) Bell Pepper; (*b*) Bird's Eye Pepper; (*c*) Long Cayenne; (*d*) Cherry Pepper

The seedlings are ready to transplant when they are 3 to 4 inches high. Plant only 2 rows in a 4-foot wide bed at a spacing of 18 inches between plants. Stake with short stakes as soon as they have been transplanted.

Correct watering is the main key to success with this crop. A moist (not wet) soil is essential. They must have sufficient water in dry spells or the plants will wilt and the effect on yields will be considerable.

Sweet peppers bear the fruits in two distinct crops, the first crop made up of large individual fruits and the second of greater numbers. To help the plant support both crops, it is advisable to give a top dressing of mixed fertiliser as soon as the first flowers open. Half a matchboxful should be sufficient, but more could be applied where the soil is either sandy or poor. This extra attention will not be wasted.

The smaller-fruited varieties like Cuban should be fruiting 2 months after planting: the larger-fruited ones will come into production about 2 weeks later.

Yields will vary according to altitude and climate, but a total crop of 40 fruits per plant of the smaller fruited and 25 from the larger-fruited should be considered good. On this basis, one bed may be enough for the average household, but it depends more on individual liking for this particular vegetable.

Chapter 3 RIDGE AND ENGLISH CUCUMBERS

THE RIDGE CUCUMBER   Cucumis sativus

The cucumber is believed to have originated in Africa and the warmer parts of Asia, but now it is grown in many parts of the world. Used mainly for salads, but also goes into cooked dishes and sauces.

It grows well from sea level to 1,000, but higher than this yields are not usually good. It is best suited to the drier areas as it is prone to attack from several of the fungus diseases, but if fungicides are used correctly it can be successful under medium rainfall. A well-drained soil is essential. Will grow well on the sandier soils if provided with fertiliser. Clay soils are not so good and they must be lightened by the application of compost or animal manure.

SUITABLE VARIETIES
Bedfordshire Prize Ridge   Palmetto
Fordhook Famous   Marketer

Plantings in high rainfall areas should be confined to the end of the rainy season and throughout the dry months. In drier areas, plantings can be made throughout the year.

After double-digging and liming (if the latter is necessary), make an application of compost or animal manure a few days afterwards. Use 4 bushels for 100 square feet and 1 lb. of mixed fertiliser at least for the same area.

Plant direct into the bed, 2 rows to a 4-foot wide bed with the seeds 2 feet apart in the rows. Do not plant the seeds more than $\frac{3}{4}$" deep because of the risk of rotting. Mulch the beds heavily so that changes in soil moisture are minimised, as these changes tend to make the vine wilt rapidly, with a consequent loss in yield. The mulch should be moved away from the seedling stems as soon as they emerge in order to lessen risk of fungus disease or insect attack.

In drier areas, the vine can be allowed to trail over the mulch. During the rains it is best to raise them off the mulch. It can be done quite simply by erecting a slatted framework over the bed, 9 inches from the ground. This not only helps to keep down fungus disease but stops the fruits from rotting. To help the vines spread rapidly over the framework, pinch out the tops when the plants are about 1 foot high. This encourages the growth of side shoots.

Cucumbers produce both male and female flowers. The male flowers usually appear first, but the females are easily distinguishable by a small swelling at the back of the flower. When the flower has been pollinated, this will swell into a fruit. If the female flowers tend to drop off, then it is advisable to hand pollinate them when the pollen is most free—that is in the middle of the day. Take a fully open male flower shake it against a female so that the pollen dust goes inside the flower.

The first cucumbers should be ready to harvest about 2 months after planting and, subject to disease attack, should go on for several months. Pick them before they start turning a paler green and you will then be picking them when the are in prime condition.

For most families, one bed will produce more than enough. You would probably do better using only half a bed.

THE ENGLISH CUCUMBER *Cucumis sativus* var. *anglicus*

This vine has a much stronger growth than the Ridge cucumber and the fruits may grow to as much as 2 feet, compared with the Ridge 8 inches. Grown mainly in England in hothouses, and is considered to be of a much better quality than the previous variety. It will thrive in drier areas in the tropics as long as it has ample supplies of compost and water.

SUITABLE VARIETY
Butcher's Disease Resistant

On a 25-foot bed place as much compost as you can spare—at least 6 bushels—in six heaps along the centre of the bed. Plant 2 or 3 seeds towards the top of each mound, pushing them in no more than 1 inch deep. The vines will need a framework erected over the bed as they must not be allowed to trail over the ground. This framework should be of the nature of a lean-to structure, rising from the ground at the front of the bed to a height of 4 feet at the back of the bed, where it will be supported by strong poles. Cross the framework with strong bamboo or palm frond ribs for the vines to be trailed over when they start to grow.

When the plants are about a foot high, remove the tips to encourage the plants to produce side shoots. From these side shoots the best cucumbers will be produced. Tie the stems to the framework and see that they are spread out as much as possible.

As with the Ridge type, both male and female flowers are produced, but with the English cucumber the male flowers *must* be removed before they are open as the female flowers must on no account be pollinated. The English cucumber is parthenocarpic, that is, it can produce a fruit without fertilisation of the female flower. The 'seeds' seen in this type of cucumber will not germinate. True seeds are only produced when the female flower is pollinated, and then the fruit produces a large swelling at the base which renders it unfit for eating.

Cucumbers are gross feeders, and this type needs a weekly dose of liquid manure to enable it to support a robust vine and later the fruit. Make liquid manure by filling a sack half full of good compost or animal manure and suspending it in a large drum of water. All the soluble plant foods will be drawn out of the manure into the water. Give this to the plants once a week. A gallon a plant should be enough. Add more water to the drum as the liquid manure is drawn off and renew the compost every month.

The English cucumber takes a little longer to come into bearing than the Ridge, but it will produce fruit for a far longer period. The fruits are ready to harvest when they are smooth throughout and still a dark green. They should be allowed to hang through the framework, if necessary supporting the lower end with raffia.

This is a crop which should only be grown by the more experienced gardeners. One bed will usually give far more fruits than can be used by the family.

Chapter 4   WATERMELON AND MUSK MELON

WATERMELON Citrullus vulgaris

The watermelon originally came from tropical Africa, but is now widely grown. Its fruit is delicious. Can only be grown to perfection in the drier areas, and it prefers the lower altitudes from sea level to 2,000 feet. Unlike most vegetables, it likes an acid soil, and a well-drained sandy type that has had fertiliser applied should produce good yields. Its cultivation should only be attempted in wetter districts where the dry season lasts for over 4 months, enabling the crop to be harvested.

Plantings in all areas should be made during the dry season.

SUITABLE VARIETIES

'Black Diamond'. A small round fruit, slightly smaller than a football, with dark green rind, deep red attractive flesh and small black seeds.

'Congo'. A long fruit, twice the size of the former, dark green rind with darker irregular stripes, flesh bright red and seeds white, with brown smears.

The nitrogen requirements of this crop are small so no compost is required; too much nitrogen can result in hollow fruits. But a good mixed fertiliser (low in N) is necessary, and should be applied at 2 lbs. per 100 square feet, forked in to the top soil.

The seeds are planted direct into the bed, one row down the centre. Plant 3 seeds every 6 feet along the row, no deeper than 1 inch.

As soon as the vines begin to run the plants will need a top dressing of fertiliser. If you have individual chemicals, use equal parts of superphosphate and muriate of potash, giving each group of plants half a pound, spread round in a ring.

Male and female flowers are produced separately, the males appearing first. If there are few pollinating insects in evidence, then it is advisable to hand pollinate. This is usually done by collecting pollen from the male flowers on a soft watercolour paintbrush and transferring it with this to the female flowers. A certain amount of care has to be taken in order to avoid damaging the flowers. Best done at midday when the sun is hottest and the pollen most free.

In many places there is no attempt made to grow watermelons, or for that matter any other melons, because the Melon Fly ruins these crops. This is rather a defeatist attitude as they can be grown, despite the Melon Fly, if both flowers and fruits are protected. As soon as a female flower

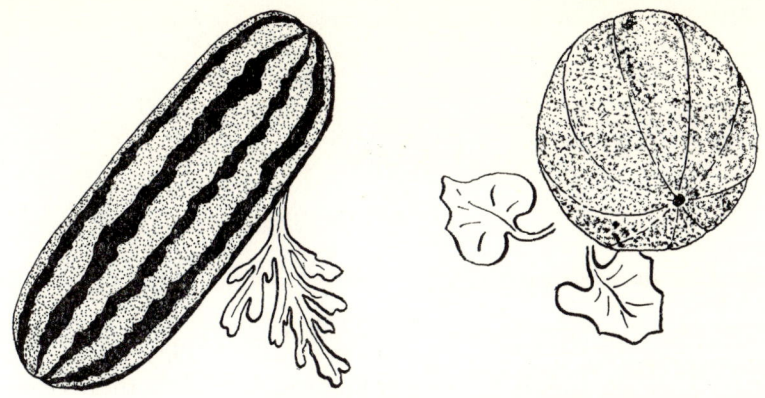

Fig. 17. *left:* Watermelon 'Congo'   *right:* Musk Melon

appears, it should be enclosed in a small bag made of mosquito netting or similar material. In some countries paper bags are used with success, but the ventilation allowed by mosquito netting is to be preferred, particularly in humid parts. When pollinating the bag must be removed, but replaced immediately. If the bag is large enough, the fruit may be allowed to develop to its full size in the bag, but otherwise it should be removed when the fruit is the size of a tennis ball.

The first fruits should be ready to harvest 3 months after planting. To test for ripeness, tap the melon in the centre sharply with the knuckles. If it produces a hollow sound it is ripe, but if not, leave for a few days.

MUSK MELON   *Cucumis melo*

The fruits of the Musk Melon are almost round, furrowed lengthways, and, if a good specimen, should weigh about 4 pounds. The flesh is orange: the seeds are congregated in the centre and not, as in the watermelon, sunk in the flesh. Difficult to grow in the tropics, except in the drier regions. The remarks already made about watermelons apply equally to this species.

SUITABLE VARIETIES

Honey Rock   Smith's Perfect

The crop is grown in the way already described for watermelon. Usually the vine will carry 4 fruits, but the pleasure of growing Musk Melon more than compensates for the small yield.

Chapter 5   OKRA AND CHAYOTE

OKRA   Hibiscus esculentus

Although okra is very widely grown and in great demand in most tropical countries, it is rarely grown as a garden vegetable. This is a great pity, as the green pods are infinitely better when freshly picked than when a few days old, when they tend to become rubbery.

It is essentially a crop for the lower altitudes and does well in humid conditions. Soil type is no real problem as it seems to grow well in acid sands and at the same time produces a reasonable crop on soils derived from limestone.

SUITABLE VARIETIES

There are two main types of okra, the Dwarf early fruiting used for commercial production, and the Tall type which takes far longer to come into bearing but continues to fruit for many months. However, as space is often an important factor in a garden, the Dwarf type is to be recommended.

Perkin's 'Long Pod', Perkin's 'Spineless', Clemson 'Spineless' and New 'Lady's Finger' are all excellent varieties which produce green pods of high quality.

Plantings can be made from the middle of the dry season onwards until the end of the rains, but water will have to be given during the dry season. Double-dig and give an application of compost or animal manure, 2 bushels to a 100 square feet and 2 lbs. of mixed fertiliser to the same area, all forked in to the top soil. Plant the seed direct into the bed. Cover with mulch in the usual way.

Okra foliage is prone to attack from beetles and other insects and spraying or dusting with the correct insecticide should begin as soon as the seedlings emerge.

About 1 month after germination, the plants will benefit from a top dressing of mixed fertiliser or, better still if you have it, nitrate of potash given at 1 lb. a bed.

You should be able to harvest young green pods after about 2 months. Do not leave them on the plant too long as they rapidly become fibrous. If they break easily at the centre, then they are in prime condition. Harvest every other day to make sure they are being gathered at their best.

One and a half beds of okra is usually enough for one family, but it would be better to make two plantings spaced six weeks apart during the season so as to have a more regular supply.

The tall type needs more room and should be planted 3 feet apart in the rows. Local selections will have to be used as there are no commercial varieties of this type.

CHAYOTE *Sechium edule*

The strong-growing vine, native of tropical America, is well known in the western tropics and deserves to be known more widely. All parts of this plant, including the perennial rootstock, are edible, but it is grown principally for the pear-shaped, grooved fruit which is used in the same way as pumpkin and marrow.

Grows best at the higher altitudes and does not seem to thrive under 1,000 feet. It can stand high rainfall but prefers medium or even low rainfall if watered well in the latter.

There are many local selections and these are propagated by cuttings in order to transmit the good characteristics. These should be used in preference to seed, but of course seed will have to be used if this vegetable is not already growing in your district.

Usually only two or three vines need be planted, as they will produce at least 50 fruits a year, and under good conditions, double this figure. Do not attempt to grow a single vine as there may be difficulties with pollination.

If you are going to use cuttings, take them at the beginning of the rains. Pieces of half-ripe stem about 1 foot in length should be planted in pots, or other suitable containers, in a sandy mixture. Place the pots in a shady position and water enough to keep the soil moist but not wet. As soon as

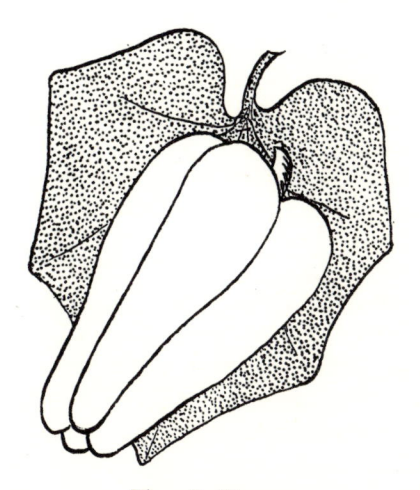

Fig. 18. Chayote

the cuttings show signs of growth they can be carefully transplanted into their permanent positions. The vines will need support as they grow to 10 feet or more—an existing fence would do. Plant the cuttings at least 8 feet apart on mounds enriched with compost.

When propagating from seed, the *whole fruit* must be planted. Plant the fruit lengthwise and cover to only half its depth; if any deeper, the seed may rot.

The first fruits should be ready after about 4 months if grown from seed, and earlier if from cuttings. Harvest will continue throughout the year.

If the plants are to be treated as a perennial, the stems should be cut back as soon as the foliage starts to die down, and a good application of compost or manure should follow.

The large root tubers are used in the same way as potatoes and are usually harvested after the plant is 2 years old.

Chapter 6 PUMPKINS, SQUASH AND MARROWS

These three are very nearly related botanically and often confused horticulturally. All receive the same cultural treatment.

SUMMER AND AUTUMN PUMPKINS *Cucurbita pepo*

Strong-growing vine with prickly stems; leaves usually large and triangular; fruits varied in size and shape and usually furrowed.

WINTER CROOKNECK PUMPKIN *Cucurbita moschata*

Soft annual vine, softly hairy; leaves usually lobed, soft and hairy with spots. Fruits oblong or crookneck.

AUTUMN AND WINTER SQUASH *Curcubita maxima*

Slightly prickly hairy vine; leaves with rounded lobes, rough, hairy and kidney-shaped; fruits round to oblong.

VEGETABLE MARROW *Cucurbita pepo* var. *condensa*

Similar to Summer and Autumn pumpkins, but also grows in bush form.

All prefer a dry climate with irrigation. The ideal is a sandy soil with a high water table, such as is found by the side of streams. Can be grown under medium rainfall, but must then be sprayed against fungus. Not too particular as to soil type, but drainage must be good.

In low rainfall areas, can be planted at the onset of the rains, but generally it is better to plant so that the vines mature during the dry season.

All may be planted direct to beds, but in dry areas they do better in sunken beds where moisture is conserved. In all cases, prepare as for Ridge cucumbers. Plant in one line along the centre of a 4-foot wide bed with a spacing of 3 feet between seeds (for the bush types) and 4 to 5 feet (trailing types). Put three seeds to a hole, and then thin out to leave the best plant when the first leaves unfold. Give a dressing of mixed fertiliser when the plants are about 6 weeks old, using 4 ozs. per plant, scattered round 6 inches from the stem.

In districts where the Melon Fly is known to exist, cover the female

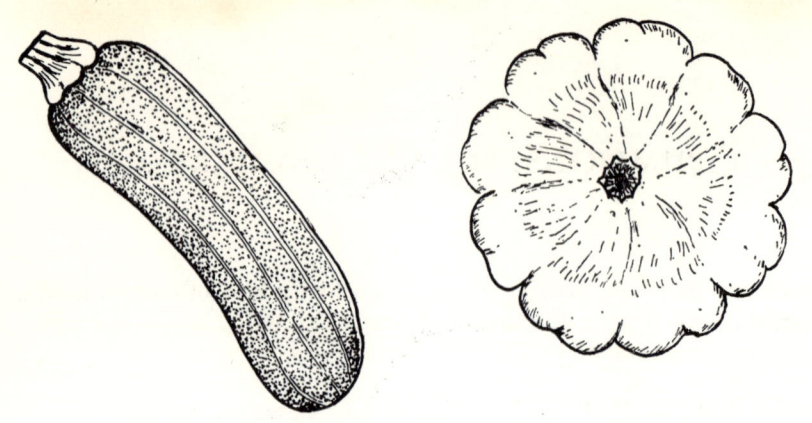

Fig. 19. *left:* Cocozelle   *right:* Summer Scallop

flowers before they open with a muslin bag, and fertilise by hand as already described for watermelon. Except in areas of low rainfall, a weekly spraying with a suitable fungicide is essential, as fungus diseases can destroy the plants in a matter of days.

It can be harvested from the small Italian types, such as 'Zuchini' about 2 months after planting. The 'Bush Scallop' also matures in about the same time. Winter Pumpkins and Squashes take longer—about 3 to $3\frac{1}{2}$ months to harvest.

Do not leave the small marrows, such as 'Zuchini', on the vine too long for they are at their best when still dark green. Winter Pumpkins and Squashes should be allowed to mature fully on the vine, and that point is reached when the stem of the fruit withers. They cannot be kept as long in the tropics as they can in colder climate.

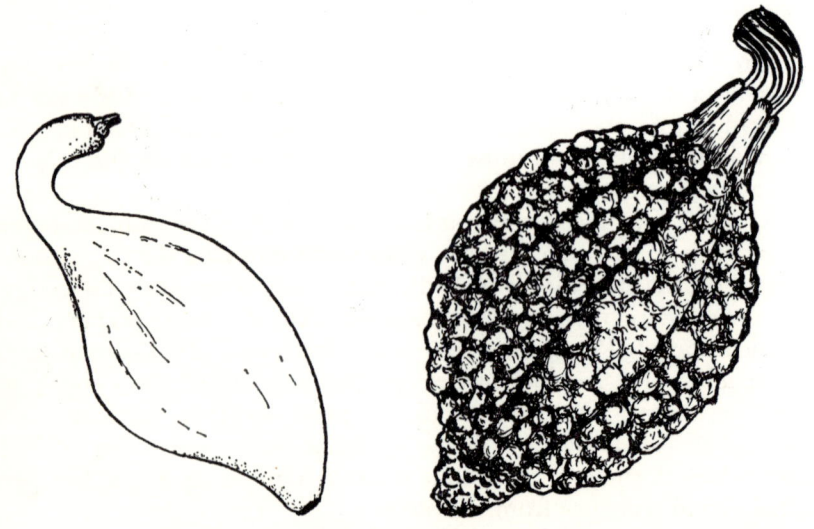

Fig. 20. *left:* Yellow Crookneck   *right:* Hubbard

SUITABLE VARIETIES

SUMMER PUMPKINS AND MARROWS 'Bush Scallop' (small, good quality pumpkin, but will not store). 'Tender and True' (bush type marrow). 'Long White Bush' (long-fruited marrow). 'Cocozelle' and 'Zuchini' (small Italian-type fruits of good quality). 'Yellow Crookneck' (small and good quality).

WINTER PUMPKINS
Striped Cushaw
Mammoth Yellow

WINTER SQUASH
Hubbard
Hundredweight

Chapter 7 OTHER INTERESTING TROPICAL GOURDS

FLUTED PUMPKIN Telfairia occidentalis

This strong-growing vine is a native of tropical Africa. It is a very useful vegetable as the young green leaves make a useful addition to the diet when others are in short supply, and the highly nutritious seeds can be stored in the fluted gourd until required.

Does best at the lower altitudes under medium to high rainfall. It will do well on the sandier soils provided fertiliser is given, but has a more robust growth in rich well-drained soil.

As this vegetable requires humid conditions, it should only be planted at the beginning of the rains. Seeds are those from the previous year which have been stored in the fluted gourd. These should not be removed until they are actually required as they deteriorate rapidly when exposed. When ready to plant, split the gourd open. Some of the seeds will probably have already started to germinate and these should be planted at once. If more seeds are wanted, place the gourd in a cool place and further seeds will germinate after a day or two.

Double-dig the beds and give a dressing of 2 bushels of compost or animal manure, forked well into the top soil. Plant the seeds 18 inches apart in rows down the centre of the bed, three seeds to a hole and not more than 1 inch deep.

It is usual to take two harvests of the young green leaves, one after a month and the second a month later. The vines should then be allowed to develop fully. Provide stout stakes as the strong tendrils of the vine will quickly grasp them for support.

The large, fluted gourds should be harvested before they are fully ripe, when they are still soft to the touch. At this stage the seeds will not have developed a hard coat, which in ripe seeds must be removed before they are cooked. The seeds are a very valuable source of protein, and can be either boiled or roasted.

One gourd should always be left to ripen fully on the vine to provide seed for the next season. This gourd should be stored off the ground on its end in a dry place. The hard rind gives adequate protection to the seed as long as it is kept dry.

(continued on page 97)

Selection of Tropical Vegetables

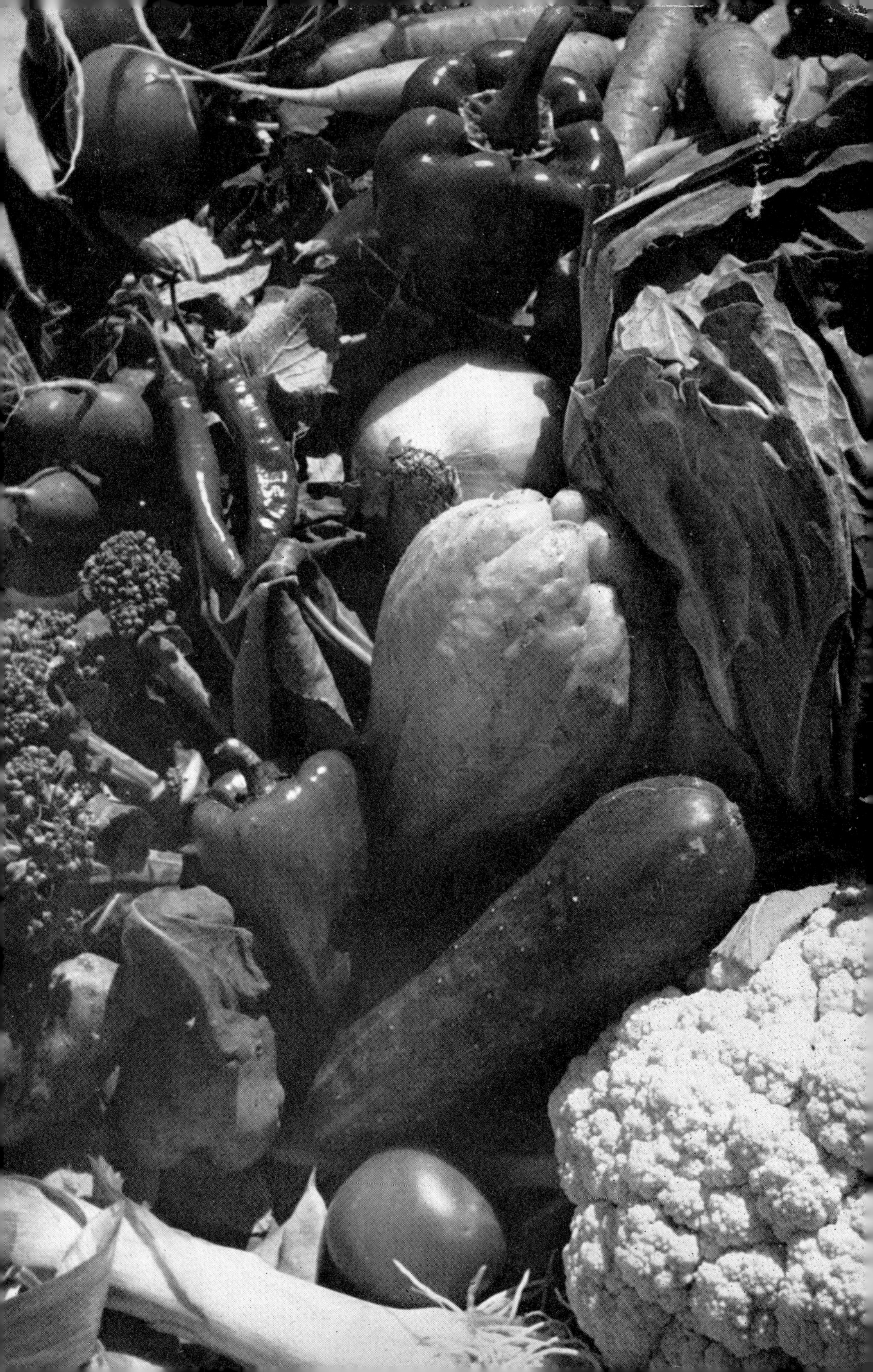

Basket of Tomato seedlings

Right: Winged Beans

French Climbing Bean – 'Kentucky Wonder'

Pole Lima Bean, *Phaseolus lunatus*

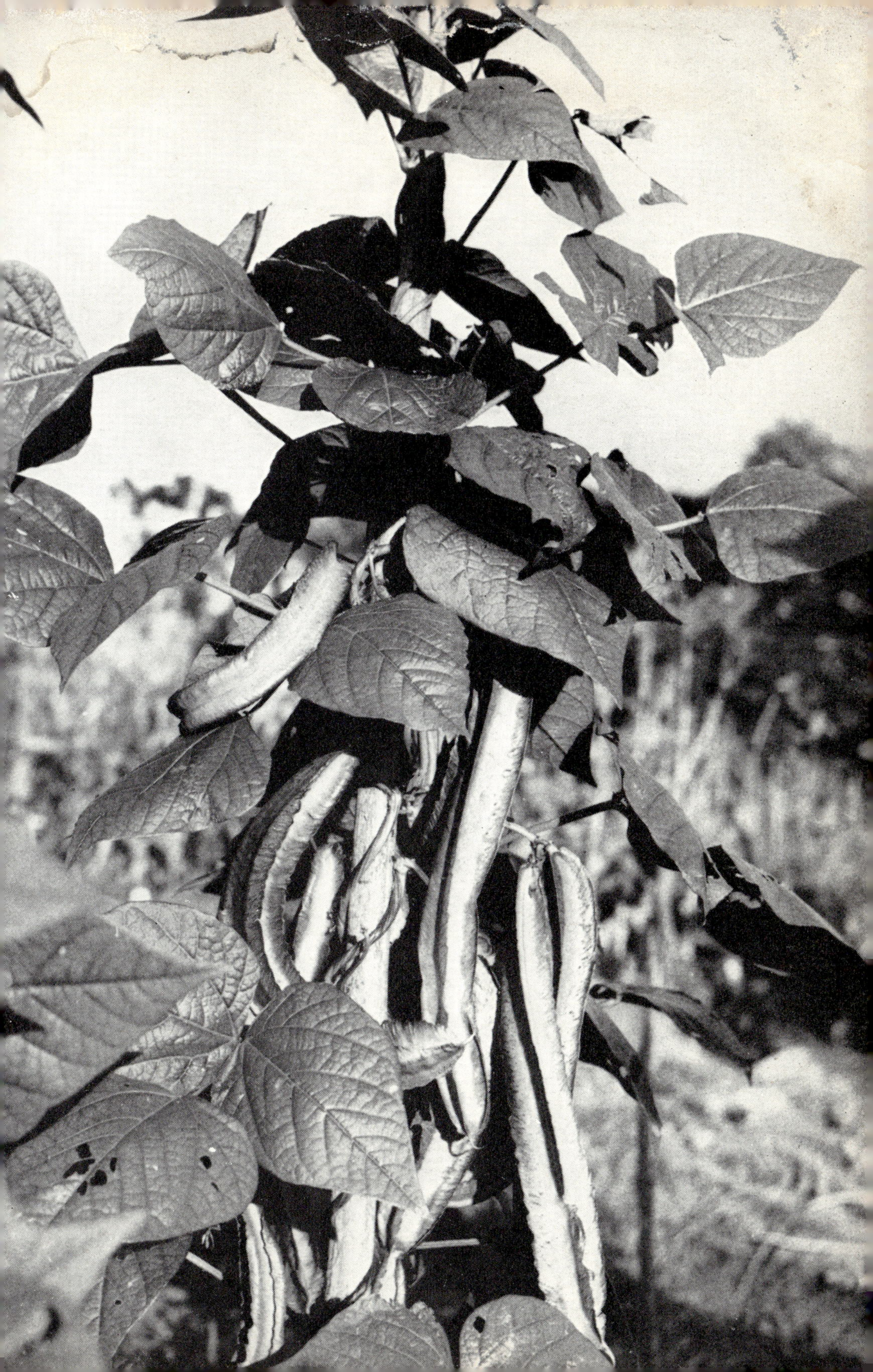

Bonavist Bean

Nematodes on Bean roots

Symptoms of virus disease on Lima Bean

Applying fertiliser to Tomato plants

Tying up Tomato plants

Garden Egg of the large
round – oval type

Leaf Miner
attack on
Tomato leaves

Downy Mildew on Cucumber

Okra Perkin's 'Long Pod'

Pickleworm damage to Cucumber fruit

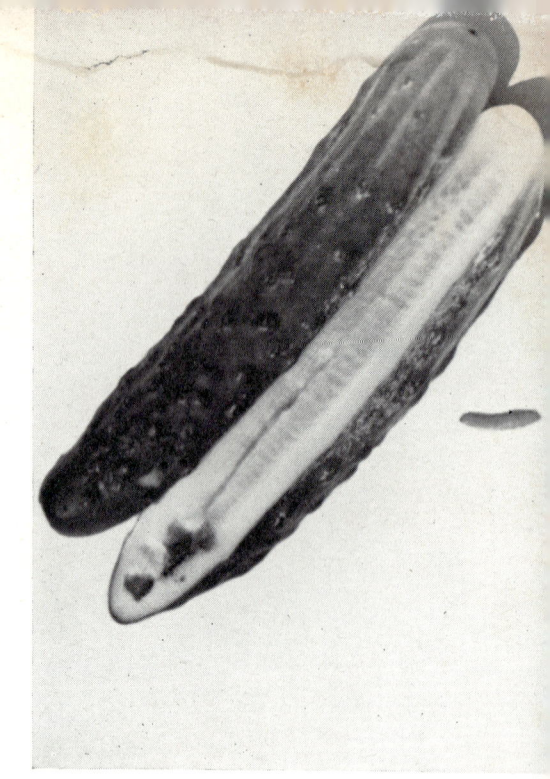

Tomato 'Dwarf Gem'

Fluted Pumpkin

Young Cucumber plants of the Ridge type

MAKING A DRILL

(i) Having raked the bed well press the stick in and continue to the end of the bed.

(ii) In a bed 4 feet wide three or four drills are made, dependent on the vegetables to be planted.

(iii) Hold the seeds in the hand and allow them to trickle through into the drill at the rate of about five seeds an inch.

(iv) Cover the seed with fine soil and replace the mulch. Do not cover the drills with mulch but leave open so that the young seedlings can grow without hindrance.

Thrip damage on Onion leaves

Beetroot 'Deep Blood-red Globe'

Tannia

Right: Cabbage
'Jersey Wakefield'

Water Leaf

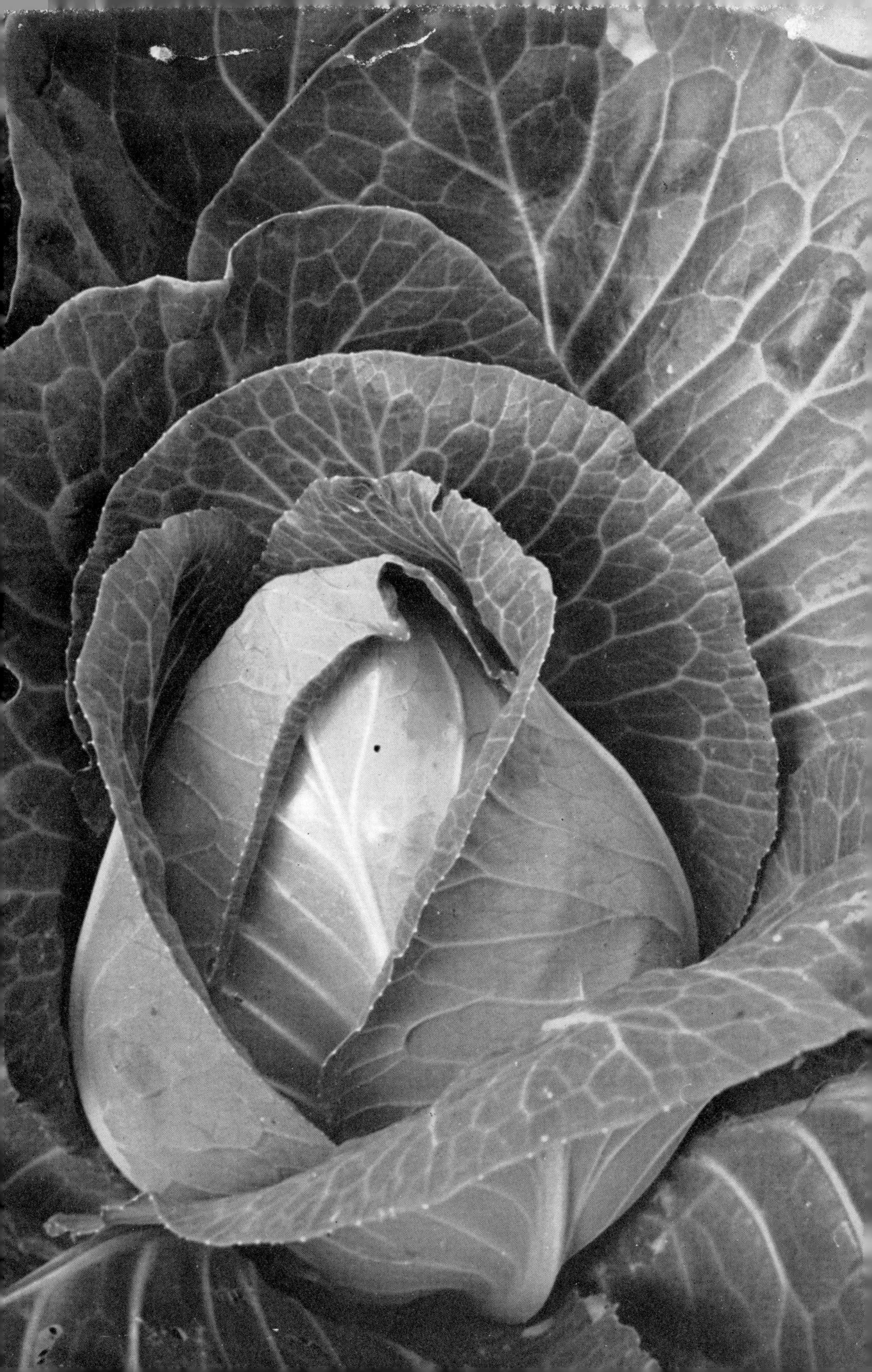

Right: Chard

Bed of Collard

Cauliflower 'Early Patna'

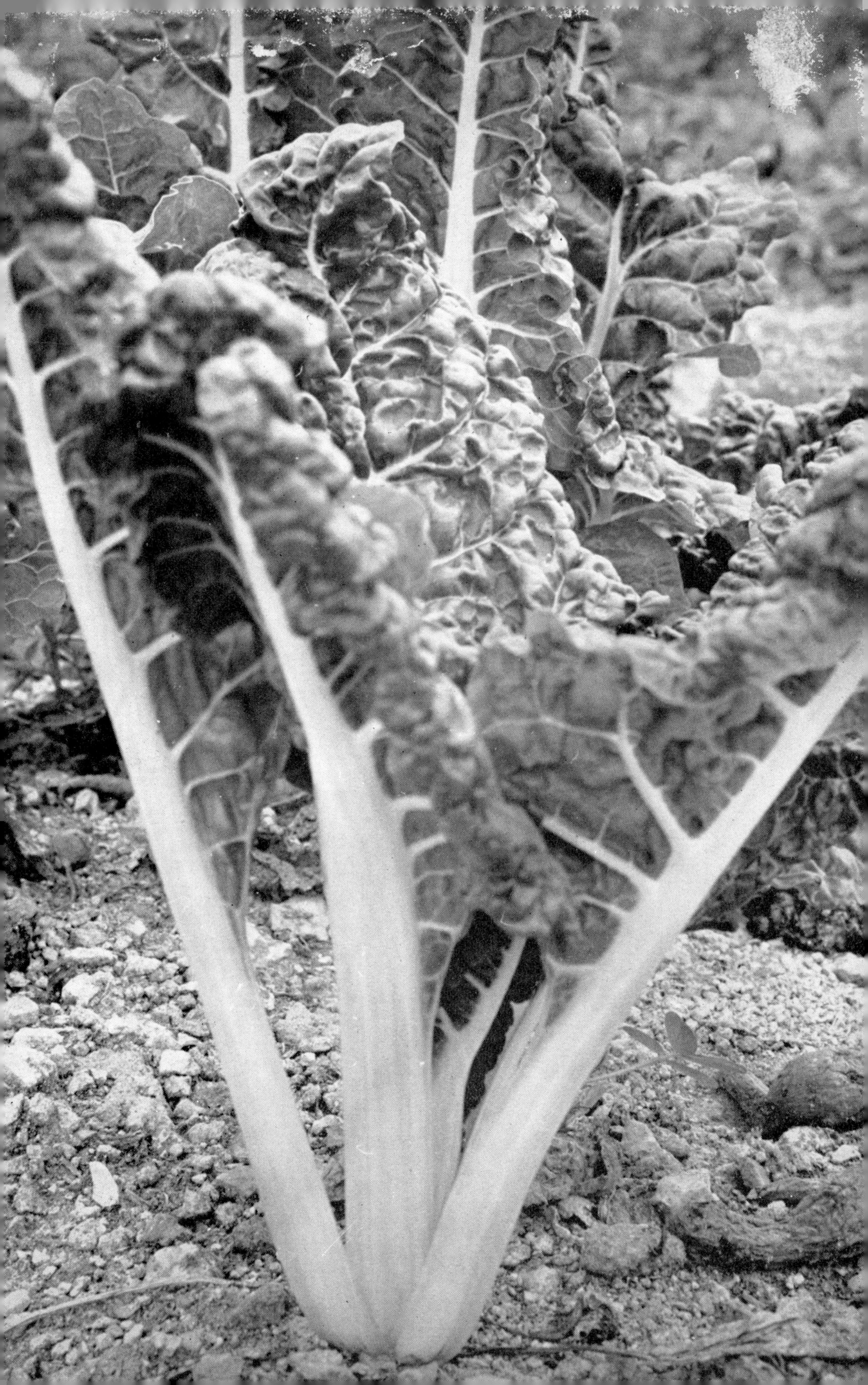

Top Left: New Zealand Spinach

Top Right: Downy Mildew on Lettuce

Above: Symptoms of Black Rot in Cabbage leaf

Blue Scotch Kale

CHINESE PRESERVING MELON *Benincasa hispida*

Common names: Chinese Preserving Melon, Ash Pumpkin, White Gourd.

Both ripe and unripe fruits of this large straggling vine are greatly appreciated by orientals. Although grown throughout the tropics, it seems rare in vegetable gardens despite the fact that it will produce melons which can keep for up to a year. Originally from tropical Asia.

Does not appear to be particular to any soil type and does well under medium to high rainfall. Is essentially a plant for the lower altitudes. Plant only at the onset of the rains.

As it is a strong climber, it is best planted against a stout fence, but otherwise it must have strong supports. Plant the seeds 18 inches apart along the centre of the bed, or against the fence. This melon does not seem to need compost, but a small top dressing of fertiliser is beneficial.

The young fruits can be harvested when about 4 lbs. in weight. They are cooked in the same way as marrows. Fully ripe gourds can weigh anything up to 40 lbs; they should be stored in a dry place until required. Like the Fluted Pumpkin, they are fully ripe when the stalk above the fruit turns dry and brown. Ripe melons are used in stews, etc.

BOTTLE GOURD *Lagenaria siceraria*

Common names: Bottle Gourd, White-flowered Gourd.

A spreading vine, originally from tropical Asia and Africa. The ripe gourds are used, as the name indicates, for bottles and water containers. Young fruits make a good substitute for young marrows, where the latter cannot be grown.

In all respects this type should be grown under the same conditions and in the same manner as already described for the Chinese Preserving Melon.

SNAKE GOURD *Trichosanthes anguina*

Common names: Snake Gourd, Guada bean, Viper Gourd, Serpent cucumber.

A large spreading vine, native of India, which produces thin, snake-like fruits which can attain a length of 6 feet. Only the young fruits are used; if allowed to ripen they become bitter. They make a good substitute for marrows or pumpkins.

Prefers lower altitudes with high rainfall. As it seems indifferent to soil type, it is invaluable in those areas where it is difficult to grow most vegetables. Treated in the same way as the Chinese Preserving Melon.

LUFFA *Luffa acutangula*

Common names: Luffa, Luffah, Dishcloth Gourd.

A strong climber, native of tropical Africa. The young gourds, which

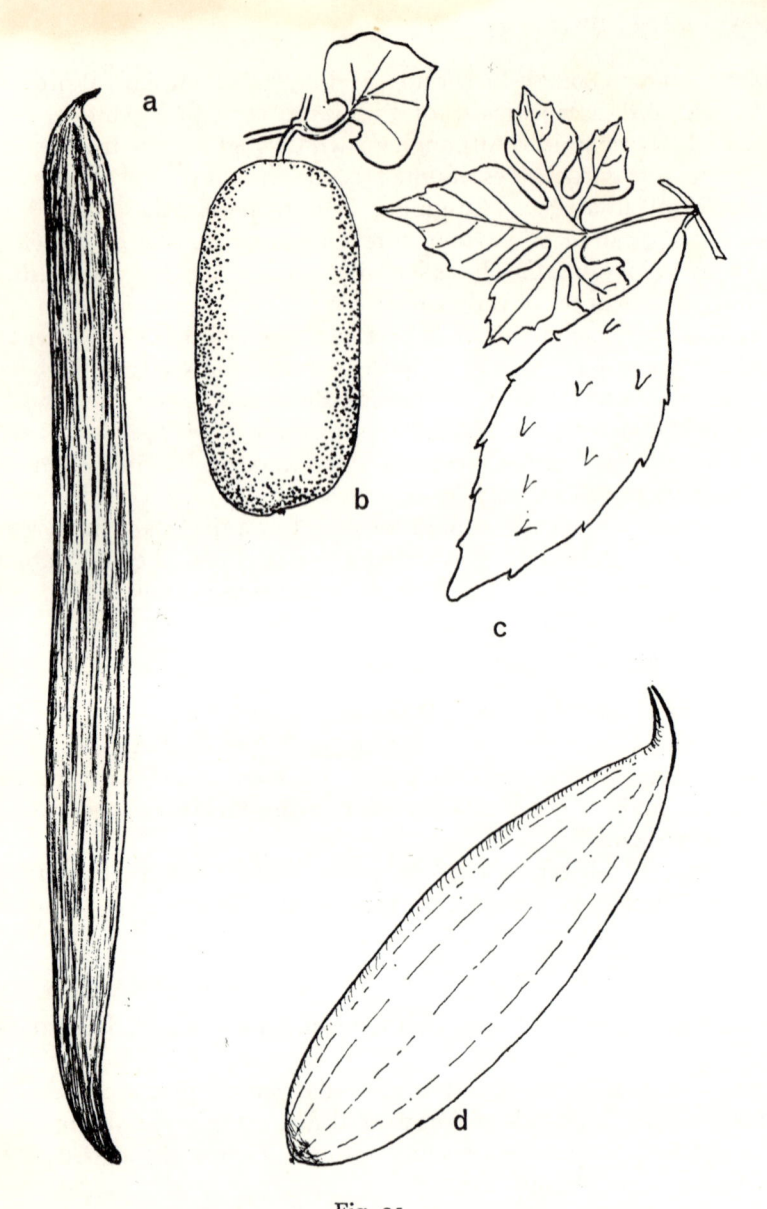

Fig. 21.
(*a*) Snake Gourd; (*b*) Chinese Preserving Melon; (*c*) Bitter Melon; (*d*) Luffa

have a slightly bitter taste, at 6 to 8 inches long can be used as a substitute for young marrows.

A plant for the lower altitude, which tolerates high rainfall but crops under much drier conditions. Does not seem particular to soil type and is therefore useful in gardens on the poorer sands. Grow as for Chinese Preserving Melon.

BITTER MELON   *Momordica charantia*

Common names: Bitter Gourd, Balsam Pear, Momordica.

A delightful spreading vine producing rich orange coloured fruits when ripe. The fruits can only be eaten when unripe and green, and have a slightly bitter taste. They grow to about 4 inches in length and are covered with spiky warts. Used with soups and meat in the same way as young marrows.

In all respects, treat as already described for the Chinese Preserving Melon.

Chapter 8   COMMON PESTS AND DISEASES OF THESE CROPS

PESTS

Never use DDT, BHC, Chlordane or Toxaphene on cucumbers, squash and melons, or Lindane on the young seedlings. Take care when using BHC on young tomato plants.

Aphids: These small white, green or black insects attack most of the vegetables in this section. They are usually seen in colonies on young growth and multiply at an amazing rate. Prompt action is essential and they should be sprayed immediately. On tomato, pepper, garden egg and okra use DDT wettable or Lindane 25% wettable, or dust the plants with Lindane or Rotenone dust. Use Lindane wettable or dust on cucumbers, melons and squash. Spraying must be systematic or further outbreaks quickly occur.

Caterpillars: Although not always seen, they do leave evidence of their presence in chewed areas in the leaves. Use DDT or Chlordane on tomatoes, peppers, garden egg and okra, but not on the fruits. Use Lindane wettable or dust, Rotenone dust or Derris dust every 10 days on cucumbers, squash, melons and for Cotton Stainer on okra.

Beetles: Garden egg is sometimes troubled with Flea beetles. These are brown, with a broad white stripe down the back, and $\frac{1}{8}$ of an inch in length. The Tobacco beetle is the same length, but cloudy black. Control by dusting with DDT or Toxaphene dust. Use Derris dust on cucumbers, squash and melons.

Mole Cricket: The Mole Cricket lives in the soil and attacks plants just below soil level; they eat through the stem and the plant collapses and dies. It can be controlled quite effectively by mixing Diazinon into the soil, but take care not to get any on the fruits as it is poisonous

Mealy Bugs: These affect most of the crops. They are found in close clusters on stems, and are usually associated with ants. Use Derris or Malathion.

Leaf Miner in Tomatoes and Peppers: The larva enters between the surfaces of the leaf and destroys the tissue, leaving a pale trail to mark its progress. In isolated cases, Lindane dust is usually effective, but if the attack is

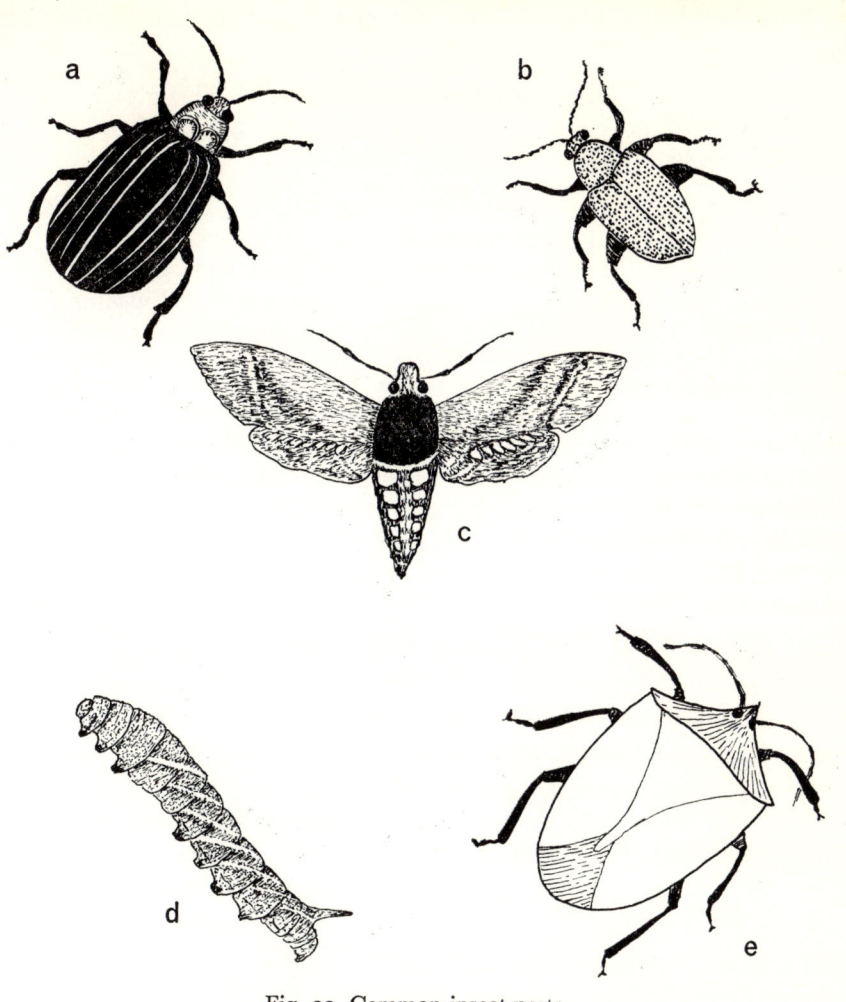

Fig. 22. Common insect pests

(*a*) Striped Cucumber Beetle (approx. $\frac{1}{3}$ inch); (*b*) Flea Beetle (approx. $\frac{1}{6}$ inch); (*c*) Protoparce Moth; (*d*) [Larva of (*c*)] Tomato Hornworm (approx. 2 inches); (*e*) Green Stink Bug (approx. $\frac{1}{2}$ inch) serious spray with Diazinon, taking care not to get any on the fruits as it is poisonous.

Tomato Fruitworms: Affects tomatoes and peppers. These pale green or brownish caterpillars eat into the pulp of the fruit, making them unusable. Dust with Derris as soon as damage is seen.

Tomato Hornworm: The larva of the large night-flying moth, *Protopace secta*, which has a wing span of 4 inches, brownish-grey wings with lighter streaks on the lower one, and five distinctive yellow spots on either side of the body. The larva has a red horn and 7 backward sweeping white stripes along the body. Use DDT dust frequently on foliage.

Stink Bugs and Plant Bugs: These can be a nuisance on okra, and sometimes on peppers. The commonest is the Southern Green Stink bug, which is pale green, shield-shaped and $\frac{1}{2}$ an inch in length. The Leaf-footed Plant bug is dark brown with a white bar across the back, and enlarged rear legs which have the appearance of leaves. It is about $\frac{1}{4}$ of an inch in length. The bugs pierce the fruit so that fungus spores can invade and ruin it. To kill them, the insects must themselves be sprayed. Toxaphene is generally used.

Mites: Minute insects like specks of dust. The Red Spider mite is sometimes found on the under side of the leaves of garden egg and other plants, usually during the dry season. Spray or dust with Malathion.

Pickleworms and Melonworms: Both will attack cucumbers and all the melons: the former, a small whitish-green grub about $\frac{3}{4}$ of an inch long attacks the fruit and the latter, a more pronounced green, feeds on the leaves only. Both have a characteristic brush of hairs at the end of the abdomen. If these pests are known to be present locally, give preventive spraying with Lindane as soon as the vines start to run. Melonworms can also be controlled by dusting the foliage with Derris.

FUNGUS DISEASES

Leaf Mould of Tomato: This fungus disease attacks the leaves and is found mostly when misty nights are followed by hot, bright days. The lower leaves are usually attacked first, browny-purple patches appearing on the under side, and the infection spreads rapidly. The areas first affected quickly turn brown as the leaf tissue dies, and as they no longer carry out the process of photosynthesis, the plant's production of new growth is therefore curtailed. There is a loss in yield and the plant may die.

In humid climates it is essential to begin spraying before the disease appears, so that a protective coating on the leaves will reduce the spread of the disease should it appear. A good programme is to start spraying as soon as the first truss appears, and then every 10 days, using either Bordeaux Mixture or a fungicide with a Zineb or Maneb base.

Leaf Spot of Tomato: Small yellow spots appear on lower leaves during humid periods. These turn brown as the tissue dies. Spreads rapidly and tends to depress yields, but rarely causes death. Preventive spraying as for Leaf Mould will lessen the danger.

Leaf Spot on peppers: Similar symptoms to tomato. Spray with Bordeaux, Zineb or Maneb compounds.

Late Blight on Tomato: Irregular-shaped yellow patches appear on the lower leaves and the affected parts rapidly turn brown. Spreads quickly and can ruin any potatoes growing near. Spray with Bordeaux or a Zineb or Maneb compound every 10 days.

Anthracnose on Garden Egg and Sweet Pepper: Keep a watch for this from the middle to the end of the rains. Yellowish circular spots appear on the leaves which later turn brown. More serious are the brown spots on the fruits, which look as though they are water soaked. This disease makes good fruit useless. Spraying against it is essential. Fortunately it can be effectively controlled. Use those sprays recommended for the previous fungus diseases. A programme systematically carried out will cover everything.

Anthracnose on Cucumbers and Melons: Small yellow areas appear on the leaves, enlarging rapidly and turning brown. Stems show oblong water-logged blisters and later they wither. Young fruits turn brown and older fruits develop cankerous spots, making them unfit to use. If the disease is widespread in your district, treat all seed with a proprietary mercury compound before planting. Spray the plants with lime-sulphur, or a Zineb or Maneb based fungicide. Bordeaux Mixture may be used on melons, but not on young plants as these may get burnt.

Fruit Rot on Garden Egg: This can be a serious disease in some districts, and here 'Black Beauty' should not be planted as it has little resistance. Circular grey spots appear on the leaves; these spread and later turn brown. There may also be a cankerous constriction of the stems, and later sunken spots appear on the fruits. In the end the plant withers and dies. Control by spraying regularly with Bordeaux.

Powdery Mildew on Cucumbers and Melons: A white powdery film appears on the upper surface of the leaves and spreads rapidly. The affected parts later turn brown. Spray every 10 days either with lime-sulphur or a Zineb or Maneb based fungicide. Flowers of Sulphur can be dusted on in the case of small attacks.

Downy Mildew on Cucumbers and Melons: Here irregular-shaped yellow spots appear on the leaves, the reverse side being brown and often covered with a purple growth. Use a Zineb or Maneb spray every 10 days from the time the vines start to run. There are now some resistant varieties.

Gummosis on Cucumber: Light brown spots appear on the older leaves, followed by shrivelling and death. Fruits and stems ooze gum. Spray with lime-sulphur or dust with Flowers of Sulphur regularly.

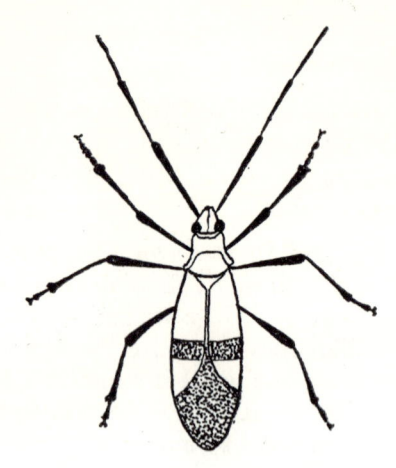

Fig. 23. Cotton Stainer Beetle

ENVIRONMENTAL DISEASES

Blossom-end Rot in Tomatoes: Most common where there is high rainfall followed by dry periods. Under these conditions water supply to the plants fluctuates considerably and the bottom of the fruit develops a dark brown scar when half grown. Keep soil moisture as even as possible by giving sufficient water during dry spells and never allowing the beds to dry out. Some authorities consider that this disease is caused by a deficiency of calcium in the soil—a condition very usual in some acid soils.

Splitting of Tomato Fruits: Very common in high rainfall areas. Two types of splitting are recognised: (1) splits appearing from under the calex (radial) and (2) splits running round the fruits (concentric). A great deal of work is being done to produce new varieties which will not split, but until these are available and have proved suitable for tropical conditions, it is better to harvest fruits just as they are turning colour. Wrap them in paper to ripen: the wrapping prevents toughening of the skins.

VIRUS DISEASES

Mosaic and Leaf-curl Viruses of Peppers: In many countries the Bird Pepper suffers from both of these. The Mosaic is distinguished by a pale mottling of the leaves and the Leaf-curl by a curling of the leaves—the centre vein appears as a keel and the two sides of the leaves resemble the sides of a canoe about it. There is no known cure, and both diseases can easily be transmitted by sucking insects from neighbouring plots or affected wild plants of the same family (*Solanaceae*) grown around. Never save seed from affected plants.

BACTERIAL DISEASES

Bacterial Wilt of Peppers: This disease can cause the death of a mature plant in a few hours. This rapid decline is a characteristic of the disease. If the stem of the dead plant is cut across, there will be seen a dark brown ring of damaged tissue. There is no cure. Plants should be dug up and *burnt*. If several cases occur in a bed, do not grow peppers, tomatoes or garden egg in that bed for several years.

IV. ROOTS, TUBERS AND BULBS

In this section will be found those vegetables which provide us with the bulk foods; many of them consist largely of starches, sugars and cellulose. These foods, the carbohydrates, provide the body with warmth and energy. Generally, they also contain a high percentage of water, but this does not detract from their value as a food.

Carrots and beet are particularly rich in sugar. The sugar (resulting from the photosynthesis which has taken place in the leaves) is stored in the thickened roots until it is required for the production of flowers and seed. The carrot is especially valuable as a source of carotene—the orange-yellow pigment which gives the root its attractive appearance. Vitamin A, which is essential to the prevention of diseases of the eye, is derived from carotene.

Chapter 1   YAMS, POTATOES AND ARTICHOKES

THE LESSER YAM   *Dioscorea esculentum*

Common names: Lesser yam, Little yam.

Of all the species of yam grown in the tropics, the Lesser yam is most suited for garden planting. The small, egg-shaped tubers are borne in great numbers at the lower altitudes where the Irish potato will not produce economically. The vine is not as robust as those of the large-tubered yams, but this is an advantage where space is limited.

Grows best from sea level to about 1,000 feet and requires a medium rainfall well distributed.

Double-dig the beds and enrich with compost or animal manure, using at least 2 bushels per 100 feet. Plantings are usually made at the beginning of the rains, but earlier plantings can be made in the dry season if the young plants can be provided with enough water until the rains begin.

Like all yams, the Lesser yam is propagated by planting tubers. Unless the crop is grown extensively in the district, when seed tubers will probably be available, tubers will have to be stored from one season to the next. They do not keep well, so this is not quite so simple as it sounds. Several storage methods have been tried. For a small quantity, the best and easiest way is to dry them well in the sun, remove all soil and tie them up in a coarse-weave sack, or bag made of fine chicken wire. Keep in a dry place secure from rodents.

Plant the tubers in 2 rows, 2 feet apart in the rows, with the upper part not more than 2 inches below the surface of the bed; it does not matter whether they are planted on end or horizontally. As soon as the first small heart-shaped leaves appear, the plants should be staked and the vines trained round. As the full-grown vine is quite heavy, strong stakes, at least 6 feet long, are necessary, pushed into the ground for $1\frac{1}{2}$ feet.

Tubers will be ready to harvest about 9 months after planting, but gather only as required; they will remain in good condition in the soil for a further 2 months, provided there is no heavy rain.

The small tubers are used in the same way as potatoes. Although the flavour is not quite as good, they make an excellent substitute.

POTATO   *Solanum tuberosum*

Common names: Potato, Irish potato, English potato.

Originated, like the tomato, from the South American Andes, and now forms an important item in diet in many countries in the sub-tropics and the temperate zones. Although it does not thrive in low coastal areas where humidity is usually high, it can be grown satisfactorily inland from 500 feet upwards. At over 3,000 feet it will produce good yields of excellent-sized tubers.

Unlike most vegetables, the potato tolerates an acid soil and there is usually no need, even on very acid types, to make an application of lime. Compost is essential and should be given as freely as possible, with a minimum of 4 bushels per 100 square feet. A dressing of good mixed fertiliser improves yields. If you are making your own mixture, use 2 parts of sulphate of ammonia, 3 parts of superphosphate and 5 parts of sulphate or muriate of potash (all by weight), and use 2 lb. per 100 square feet of bed. Both compost and fertiliser should be raked into the top soil.

The potato can be propagated either by tubers or cuttings; the former is normal when first starting to grow the crop, but afterwards cuttings can be taken from existing stocks.

It will be noticed that the tubers have 'eyes' from which sprouts will probably be emerging. Take care not to break these off when planting as they later grow into stems and foliage. If the seed tubers are very expensive, large ones can be cut into two or three pieces as long as there is an 'eye' in each piece. But if cut, the pieces must be planted as once and not allowed to dry out; if they do dry out they will probably not survive.

Plant them 2 feet apart in the rows, with 2 rows to a 4-foot wide bed, and not more than 6 inches below the surface: in the wetter areas they might rot. With good tubers, growth above ground should be seen within 10 days of planting.

When about 6 inches high, the soil on either side of the row should be moved towards the plant to form a ridge. This brings the soil above the area around each plant and stops the tubers, as they swell, from pushing out of the ground. If tubers do become exposed, the skin becomes green and that part is unusable.

They should be ready to lift about 4 months after planting, but before doing so, scrape away some of the soil round a plant to check if the tubers are a good size. If not, leave for a few days. Lift with a fork. They do not keep very well in the tropics, so only lift enough for immediate needs.

Once a stock has been established, cuttings from the plants can be taken for another bed. Take young shoots about 4 inches long and plant at once. The best planting time is at the middle of the rains. Keep shaded for a few days to prevent excessive wilting.

Many varieties have been tried out in the tropics and some are still being grown although their names are forgotten. If any such are available and yield well, they should be used. Otherwise the following commercial varieties might be considered:—

'Arran Pilot', 'Epicure', Bliss 'Triumph', 'Irish Cobbler'.

SWEET POTATO *Ipomoea batatas*

Common names: Sweet potato, Spanish potato.

Although widely grown in the tropics, the sweet potato is often considered to be a poor quality food. This is not so: it contains a higher percentage of vitamins A and B than does the Irish potato, and has the added attraction of producing edible leaves. Texture and flavour can vary considerably, but recognised commercial varieties are excellent.

It is an ideal crop for gardens in low coastal belts where rainfall may be high, or in drier parts where the watertable is high and the soil remains moist. Though more generally grown at the lower altitudes, it is quite successful up to 5,000 feet, but in these parts the Irish potato is usually preferred.

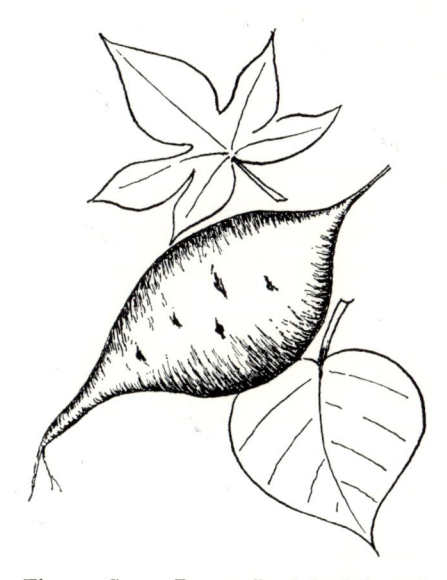

Fig. 24. Sweet Potato (both leaf shapes)

If fertiliser is supplied, it can do without compost. Too much compost or animal manure in the soil tends to produce an abundance of foliage to the detriment of tuber formation. Apply a good mixed fertiliser, rich in potash, before planting. If such a mixture is not available, use the normal mixture and give a dressing of woodash.

There are several hundred varieties and countless local selections. It is better to use local selections if the flavour and texture is to your taste. Of the commercial varieties, 'Nancy Hall' produces large tubers swollen at the centre with a deep yellow flesh. 'Puerto Rico' produces tubers of a more irregular shape with yellow flesh.

Plantings are usually made at the beginning of the rains for a main crop with, possibly, a further planting at the end of the rains to carry on into the dry season.

There are three methods of propagation: pieces of tuber, 'slips' (shoots broken off the tuber) and softwood cuttings. Of the three, the last is probably most widely used.

To produce 'slips', tubers must be planted well before the normal time, in a bed of sand, and well watered to make them produce shoots. Carefully break off the shoots against the tuber as soon as they emerge, and plant into the bed at once.

Softwood cuttings are taken from plants previously established—perhaps from a bed planted at the end of the rains and kept watered during the dry season—and should not be more than 12 inches in length. Plant at an angle of 45° with two-thirds of the cutting below the soil. If no rain has fallen, water well before planting as the soil must be moist. If kept watered, the cuttings should show signs of growth within 2 weeks. Any that do not should be replaced with fresh cuttings.

Whatever method is used, plant 15 inches apart in one row down the centre of a 4-foot wide bed.

Maturity varies with varieties, but most will be ready from 4 to 6 months after planting. Mature tubers do not show green on the skin or on cut surfaces. They do not keep well, so lift only as required. Store, if you are keeping some, in dry sand in a rodent-proof container.

JERUSALEM ARTICHOKE   Helianthus tuberosus

Common names: Jerusalem Artichoke, Girasole.

A perennial herb from North America. Its common name 'Jerusalem Artichoke' is said to be a corruption of the Italian 'Girasole', and has no connection with the city. The tubers are rich in carbohydrates in the form of anulin and not starch, which should make them particularly attractive to people watching their weight. It is not a tropical subject, but is grown in many tropical countries. While highest yields are obtained at the high altitudes, good crops of smaller tubers may be had as low as 500 feet. Needs a rich soil, with applications of compost and fertiliser. Should be planted during the rainy season.

Varieties of French origin, such as 'Fuseau' are far the best in texture and flavour, and the tubers are not as irregular as the more common types.

Beds should be double-dug, with compost at the rate of 2 bushels per 100 square feet and 1 lb. mixed fertiliser for the same area forked into the top soil.

Plant the tubers horizontally not more than 3 inches deep 18 inches apart in the rows, with 2 rows to a 4-foot wide bed. Heavily mulch after planting. The young plants should appear in about 2 weeks; they will grow as high as 8 feet, but usually much less at the lower altitudes. Flowers of the small sunflower type are produced after 5 months, and when these and the foliage have died down, the tubers will be ready to harvest.

Once lifted, the tubers do not keep well, and only as many as are required should be lifted at a time. As they will mature in the dry season, the tubers can be left in the ground where they will remain dormant as long as there is little moisture.

Some people think the tubers rather 'soapy', so it is as well to check they are liked before making any large plantings. Use as you would potatoes, for which they are an excellent substitute in the lower altitudes where potatoes do not thrive.

Chapter 2 CARROTS, BEETROOT, WHITE TURNIP AND RADISH

CARROTS Daucus carota

Common names: Carrot, Kaloke.

A biennial herb originating from Europe. The thickened root has been used for food or medicine for centuries. If the correct varieties are used, it can be grown at all altitudes in the tropics. The longer-maturing, longer-rooted varieties are best suited to the cooler conditions of high lands, and the quick-maturing, smaller roots do best at the lower altitudes. Best results come with a well-distributed medium rainfall: there is less danger of loss through 'Leaf Blight' than in areas of higher rainfall. Carrots like a free sandy soil which has not recently had compost applied. A soil high in humus tends to produce hairy roots.

In high rainfall areas, best results will be obtained from plantings made at the end of the rains. Elsewhere, plantings can usually be made throughout the year, provided water can be given during dry periods.

SUITABLE VARIETIES	LOW TO MEDIUM ALTITUDES	HIGH ALTITUDES
	Chantenay	Danver's Half-long
	Early Nantes	Intermediate
	Cape Market	

After double-digging, rake down the top soil to produce as fine a tilth as possible. Do not apply manure or compost, but if the previous crop received compost, this will not adversely affect the roots. Work mixed fertiliser at the rate of 1 lb. for every 100 square feet of bed into the top soil.

The seeds are best sown in drills, direct to the bed. A drill is a shallow trough made along the length of the bed, about $\frac{1}{2}$ an inch deep—see the illustrations on page 90. Seed should be sown thinly. It is wasteful to sow thickly as later all surplus plants will have to be removed. It is not easy to sow thinly as it is very small. The easiest way is to mix the seed with fine sand; the mixture will be quite easy to control as it is allowed to trickle out of the hand into the drill. A 4-foot wide bed will take three drills. Cover the seed with fine soil and mulch the ground between the drills. Water must be given during the dry season in order to promote quick growth. Water between the rows and leave it to percolate through to the roots.

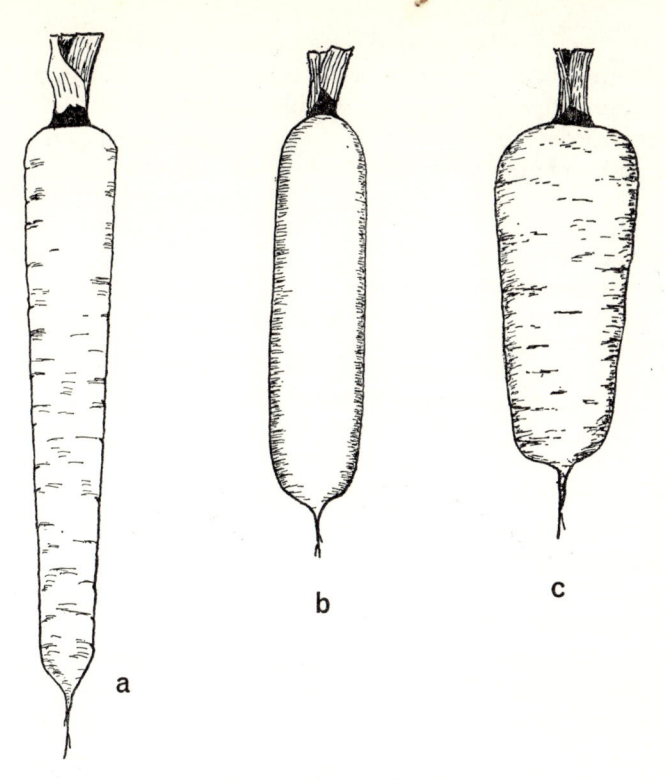

Fig. 25. Carrot shapes
(*a*) Intermediate; (*b*) Nantes; (*c*) Chantenay

When the seedlings are about 3 inches high, thin them to leave one good plant every 2 to 3 inches along the row. Make the soil firm around the remaining plants. During the rains, young plants removed by thinning can be transplanted into other beds, but this is hardly worth doing in the dry season.

The young roots can be harvested in about $2\frac{1}{2}$ months. Sometimes roots will raise the crowns above the soil, and the crowns should be covered again or they will become green.

If popular with the family, it would be advisable to make a planting every 4 to 6 weeks throughout the season.

BEETROOT Beta vulgaris

Common names: Beetroot, Red Beet, Beet.

A biennial herb, native of Europe, which can be grown in most places in the tropics. Larger roots are produced at the higher altitudes, but even at sea level the smaller ones can be of a very good quality, and useful not only in salads but as a hot, cooked vegetable. Beetroot tolerates high rainfall, but prefers less humid conditions. It needs a well-drained soil, rich in humus and not excessively acid. Acid soils should be given a dressing of lime when the beds are double-dug.

The biggest roots come with plantings made during the rains, but plantings can be made during the dry season where there can be adequate watering.

SUITABLE VARIETIES

There are two main types of beetroot—the globe-rooted and the long-rooted. The former is to be preferred as it matures more quickly than the latter and is of a far superior quality.

LOW AND MEDIUM ALTITUDES	HIGH ALTITUDES
Deep Blood-red Globe	All mentioned and
Crimson Globe	Crosby's
Detroit Dark Red	'Egyptian'

Apply compost at the rate of 2 bushels per 100 square feet and mixed fertiliser at 1 lb. for the same area. Work the top soil into a fine tilth by raking out all lumps and stones, and then smooth level.

Sow the seed in drills, as has already been described for carrots. Beet seed often gives poor germination, so buy either fresh or seed that has been stored in sealed packets. If the seeds are soaked for a day before planting, they will germinate more quickly. As the individual seed is quite large, space them about $\frac{1}{2}$ an inch apart along the drill and not more than $\frac{1}{2}$ an inch deep, 3 drills to a 4-foot wide bed. Cover with fine soil and mulch between the drills. Thin out when about 3 inches high, leaving a strong plant every 3 inches along the row. These thinnings are not suitable for transplanting.

Most varieties will be ready to harvest from about 2 months after planting. Lift the roots carefully and lay in full sun to dry. This toughens the skin and the root will not 'bleed'. The green and purple tops can be cut off and cooked as a vegetable. Surplus beetroots can be preserved in vinegar.

One bed should be sufficient for the requirements of most families.

WHITE TURNIP *Brassica rapa*

There are several types of turnip, but only the one producing a white tuber is suitable for the tropics as the others fail to produce good roots, even at high altitudes. The White Turnip can be grown from sea level upwards. It produces a globe-shaped root, either all white, or with the upper part of a darker colour.

Quick growth is essential for the production of good quality roots; if the plants are checked by drought the roots become woody and unpalat-

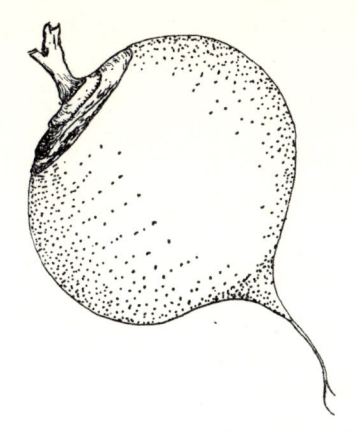

Fig. 26. White Turnip 'Early Snowball'

able. Compost and fertiliser are therefore necessary, as is also double-digging to ensure good drainage. Plant during the rains. Unless the turnip is a great favourite, half a bed planted every month will give an adequate supply.

Sow in drills, as for carrots, spacing only 2 or 3 seeds per inch along the drill. Cover with fine soil and mulch between the drills.

When about 3 inches high, thin out to leave one good plant every 3 to 4 inches. The leaves of the thinnings can be used as a green vegetable.

Start pulling the roots as soon as they are $1\frac{1}{2}$ inches in diameter for, if left too long, too many will be ready at one time and some will have become 'woody'. The green leaves of the mature turnip can also be used as a vegetable.

SUITABLE VARIETIES

Early Snowball   Purple Top White Globe

RADISH *Raphanus sativus*

The radish is well known throughout the world. It grows all through the tropics and under all kinds of rainfall.

SUITABLE VARIETIES

There are 2 main types, those with long roots and those with globe-shaped roots; the latter are to be preferred for the tropics.

Crimson Globe, Scarlet Globe, French Breakfast.

The crop is easy to grow and is therefore often not given the minimum of attention, with the result that maximum yields are not obtained. Like most vegetables it benefits from an application of compost and fertiliser. Give 2 bushels of the former and 1 lb. of the latter of a good mixture to

100 square feet. Drill 4 rows to the bed, and more thickly than carrots. Do not make the drills any deeper than $\frac{1}{2}$ an inch. Cover the seed and mulch between the rows.

Harvest as soon as the roots are about $\frac{1}{2}$ an inch in diameter. They will grow much bigger than this but develop a rather pungent flavour which some people do not like. If used a lot, radish can be planted at 2- or 4-week intervals, half a bed at a time to provide a good supply of the finest quality all the time.

Chapter 3 ONIONS, LEEKS AND SHALLOTS

ONION Allium cepa

Common names: Onion, Bulb onion.

Onion cultivation is known to date back to the Egypt of the Pharaohs, and is almost surely more ancient than that. Today it is in demand in even the smallest markets, and always seems to command a good price. Its production is generally very localised. This is rather strange, for the right variety, planted at the right season and given suitable fertiliser, will produce reasonable results even under the most unlikely conditions. The highest yields and best quality bulbs come from 1,000 feet upwards, but reasonable crops can, and have been obtained at much lower levels. Where rainfall is medium to heavy in a clearly defined season, onions are best planted in the middle of the period so that they can take full advantage of the moisture for the early vegetative growth, but develop the bulb and ripen it in the drier months. In drier areas, plant at the onset of the rains. In the highlands, autumn plantings will give the best results.

A rich, well drained soil is best, but sandy soils are good if suitably fertilised. Compost is advisable, but do not use more than 2 bushels per 100 square feet, for an excess of nitrogenous matter in the soil spoils results. Equal parts of sulphate or muriate of potash and superphosphate can be applied at the rate of 2 lb. for the same area, forked into the top soil. Break down the top soil to a really fine tilth, removing all lumps and stones. Then firm down by placing a board on top of the bed and walking on it. Onions do not like a loose soil.

SUITABLE VARIETIES

'Yellow Bermuda' or 'Excel'. (A medium-sized thick flat bulb of mild flavour; does not keep very well.) 'Texas Grano.' (A large bulb, bigger at the top than at the root end, straw coloured skin with white flesh. A good keeper if properly dried.) 'Red Kano.' (An excellent West African type, medium-sized bulb with red skin and pale pink flesh.) 'Red Patna.' (Medium size, globe-shaped bulb, with red skin and pale pink flesh. Mild flavour.)

The seed may be planted either direct into the bed, in drills, or first into a seedbox and transplanted when the young plants are about 3 inches high. The first method is probably more convenient for gardeners, but the seed must be sown very thinly in the drills. Thin when the plants are a few inches high and use the thinnings as Spring onions in salads. Leave about 8 inches between plants, and firm the soil around each one, but take care not to press them into the ground.

As the plants grow some may develop stems that are far thicker than normal. Watch these carefully as they may 'bolt' and produce flowers. If flowers are produced, there will be no bulbs. Even so, they are still useful in cooking if pulled before the flower stem emerges. As the plant develops, bulbs form, generally above the ground. Leave to grow in this way. If the bulbs are closely mulched or earth is pushed round them, they can quite easily rot before they are ripe. Also, do not cultivate between the rows more than is necessary to clear weed growth as, once the bulbs begin to form, onions do not like having the soil disturbed.

As the bulbs mature the tops of the green leaves wither and eventually die down completely. This is the time to lift the bulbs: leave them lying in full sun with the dead tops still on them. If the weather is humid, take them inside or cover them up before it is dark, and put them out again next morning. If thoroughly dried, the bulbs will keep for some time. When they are completely dry, the outer skin rustles and tends to flake off, and the tops should then be wrung off, dry roots removed and the bulbs stored in a dry place. One of the best methods of storing is to keep them in a bag made of small-gauge chicken wire suspended from the roof of a store. Onions grown in the drier areas keep the longest.

Most varieties take from 5 to 6 months to mature. Usually one sowing will provide enough for several months' supply. Because they store much better in the drier areas, here it may be desirable to make an extra sowing, 2 to 3 weeks after the main one.

EGYPTIAN ONION   *Allium cepa* var. *aggrigatum*

Common names: Egyptian onion, Tree onion.

This type grows in much the same way as the previous one, but young onions are produced in clusters at the apex of the flower cluster. More suited for the drier areas.

Propagate by planting young bulbs harvested from the head of an old plant. Can be propagated sometimes by young bulbs produced about the mother bulb. Plant out in beds prepared as for bulb onions. Space 6 inches apart in the rows, with 3 rows to a 4-foot wide bed.

The plants should flower after about 6 months. The young onions can be harvested green, when they are useful for salads, or allowed to ripen on the plant, when they can be kept for a short time.

WELSH ONION   *Allium fistulosum*

Common names: Welsh onion, Spring onion.

This onion produces a cluster of shoots, each developing a small bulb.

It is used mainly as a salad onion as the bulbs are small.

It is propagated by splitting up a clump carefully and planting the individual bulbs about 1 foot apart. As new shoots are produced they can be harvested, leaving the main clump to continue producing more shoots. It is advisable to leave the main clumps undisturbed for several years, giving an occasional dressing of compost to promote fresh growth.

SHALLOT form of *Allium cepa*

Common names: Shallot, Red onion.

The shallot is much prized and has a milder flavour than most onions. The small, angular bulbs grow out from around the base of the mother bulb and remain attached to it.

It thrives in the drier climates at medium altitudes. Does not do well below 1,000 feet or under high rainfall.

Usually the mature bulbs are planted out, from which will develop rings of bulbs, but they can be grown from seed if no mother bulbs are available locally. Plant the seed in a seedbox and transplant into beds (prepared as for onions) when the seedlings are from 3 to 4 inches high. Space 6 to 8 inches apart in the rows with 3 rows to a 4-foot wide bed. Use the same spacing for bulbs if you can get them.

The clusters of bulbs will be ready to harvest when the foliage has fully dried out, about 5 months after planting the bulbs, or a little longer if planting from seed. After lifting, complete the drying in full sun, and do not allow them to get damp at any time. When properly dried they will keep for several months. Usually, however, they are put to use immediately and pickled, either alone with spices, or with other vegetables such as pieces of cauliflower 'curd'.

LEEK *Allium porrum*

The leek undoubtedly was known and esteemed by the ancient Egyptians. The Romans, too, thought highly of it and considered that leek soup taken daily produced a sonorous voice suitable for oratory. It is widely grown, except in the tropics. This is rather strange as it will grow reasonably well under most conditions. It is at its best at the higher altitudes: from sea level to 1,000 feet it may not grow much thicker than a pencil, but it will grow and makes an excellent substitute for onions when they are in short supply.

At all altitudes, plantings made at the end of the dry season and at the beginning of the rains should produce the largest leeks.

SUITABLE VARIETIES

Mussleburgh   Italian Giant   Large American Flag

Plant the seeds either in seedboxes or in small drills, as for onions. Prepare the beds, too, as for onions.

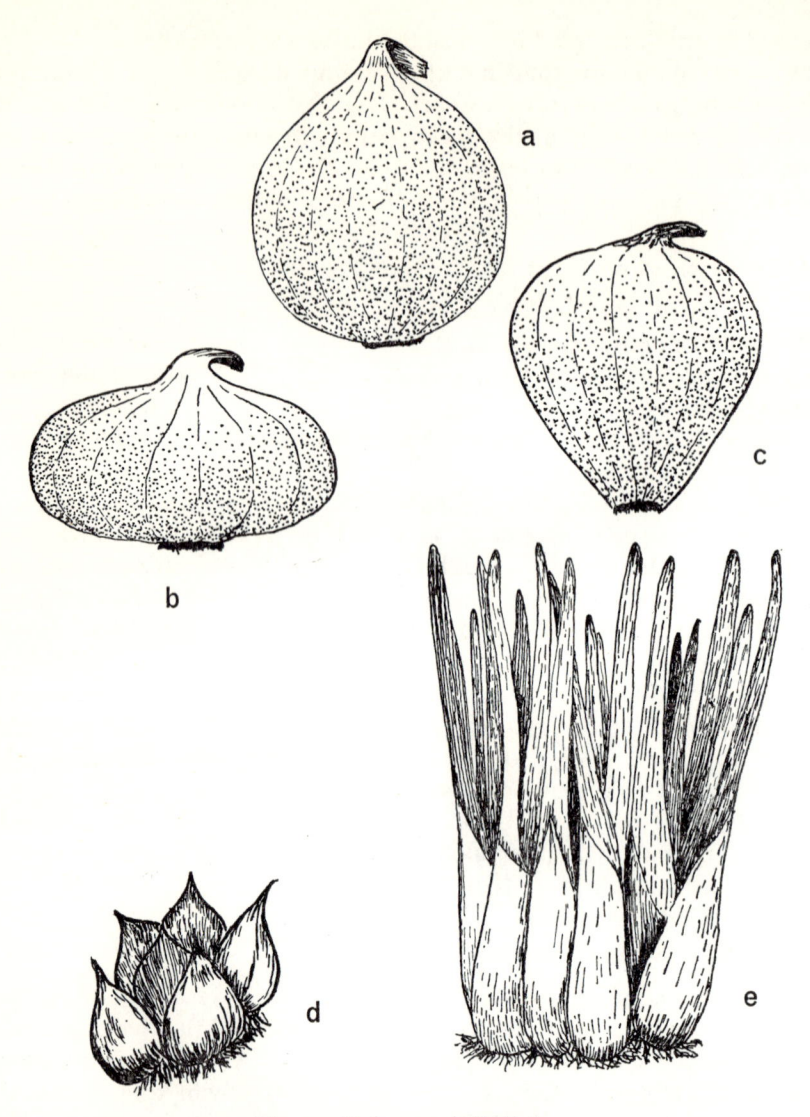

Fig. 27. Onions and Shallots
(a) Patna; (b) Bermuda; (c) Grano; (d) Shallots; (e) Welsh Onion

When the seedlings are 3 to 4 inches high, transplant into the beds 9 inches apart in the rows, with 3 rows to a 4-foot wide bed. Plant them lower than they were growing in the seedbox, sinking them at least an inch into the soil. This ensures that the stem, which is the important part, will be blanched over a greater length. As the plants grow, draw up the soil round each one in order further to increase the blanched length, but do not draw the soil up any farther than where the leaves break out from the stem.

They mature in from $4\frac{1}{2}$ to 5 months and will keep well in the bed if not allowed to become too dry.

Chapter 4   OTHER INTERESTING ROOT VEGETABLES

SALSIFY AND SCORZONERA   *Tragopogon porrifolius* and *Scorzonera hispanica*

Common names: Salsify, Oyster plant, Vegetable Oyster.   Scorzonera, Black Salsify.

These will only produce roots of a good size at the higher altitudes; elsewhere foliage will be obtained, but the plants usually run to seed quickly. The roots are a delicacy, the former is white and the latter black-skinned. They are in shape rather like a carrot and used similarly, but after peeling they must be soaked in water to remove the slightly bitter taste.

Both are grown from seed, which should be planted at the beginning of the rains in the same way as carrots. The roots take about $2\frac{1}{2}$ months to mature.

CHINESE ARTICHOKE   *Stachys tuberfera*

Common names: Chinese Artichoke, Crosnes, Chorogi.

This perennial root vegetable from China is not known widely in the

Fig. 28. Salsify

tropics. The curiously-shaped tuberous rhizomes are constricted to form a bead-like chain, and are produced in profusion just beneath the surface of the soil. Eaten raw, they taste rather like a radish, but can be cooked and used in the same way as Jerusalem artichokes.

They do best at the lower altitudes where, if planted in a rich soil, the roots may grow as long as 2 feet in six months.

Plant the tubers 6 inches apart in the rows, with three rows to a bed, at the beginning of the rains is the best time to do so.

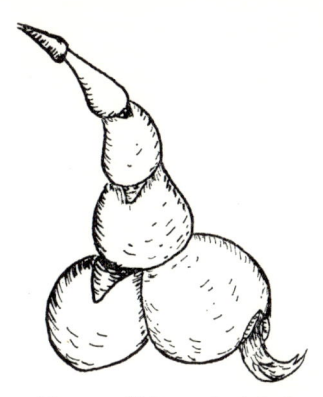

Fig. 29. Chinese Artichoke

EDDO *Colocasia esculenta*

Common names: Eddo, Coco-yam, Taro, Dasheen.

In some tropical countries Eddo is of great importance, and is a major source of carbohydrates, minerals and vitamins A and B. The tubers of the better selections are of reasonable quality. They can be either boiled or baked, and the young shoots, stalks and leaves can be used as a leaf vegetable.

This is essentially a plant for the lower altitudes and needs moist conditions. Some selections do well planted beside streams, whilst others prefer drier land under heavy rainfall.

Propagation is by dormant buds, whole tubers or the top of the tuber with shoot sprouted. Best planted in the rainy season, for the plants must not be allowed to dry out. Planting distance is determined by the richness of the soil, anything from 30 to 36 inches apart. Plant not more than 3 inches from the soil surface, and then mulch all over to preserve soil moisture.

Harvest can start about 6 months after planting. The tubers do not keep well and only sufficient should be lifted for immediate purposes.

TANNIA *Xanthosoma sagittifolium*

Common names: Tannia, Malanga, Yautia.

Something like Eddo, but the large leaves are arrow shaped whilst those of Eddo are heart shaped. The main tuber is often too acrid in taste and only the smaller ones growing from it are used. Another species, *X. violaceum*, 'The Blue Taro', is grown throughout the West Indies, Central America and parts of Africa. Leaf stems and veins are violet. It is grown in the same way as Eddo, but the tubers may take 9 months to mature.

Chapter 5 PESTS AND DISEASES OF THESE CROPS

Aphids: These small, white, green or black insects can infest many of the crops in this section. They will usually be observed in clusters, often on young growth. As they multiply at an alarming rate, immediate action must be taken or they will spread to all crops. They are particularly dangerous as they help to spread many of the virus diseases. Can usually be controlled by spraying with Malathion every 10 days.

Beetles: Hard-shelled black beetles attack the Irish potato, damaging the foliage. They are very difficult to kill, except with a very poisonous spray, and it is really far better to spray with Bordeaux Mixture, which will probably be to hand for use against fungus diseases, as this has repellent qualities.

Tortoise Beetles: Attack Sweet potatoes They are easily identified by their bright colours. The Golden Sweet Potato beetle is the most striking—a brilliant metallic gold with a bluish sheen. They are about $\frac{1}{4}$ inch long, with a characteristic fringe, and sometimes spotted with black on the back. Spray or dust with Toxaphene.

Sweet Potato Weevil: This pest can be devastating. The adult beetle is about $\frac{1}{4}$ inch long, slender, head black and body and legs a bright red. The white grubs eat into tubers rendering them inedible. Breeding is continuous throughout the year. Burn all potato stems and foliage after harvest.

Nematodes: Eelworms can be a nuisance on most crops, making boil-like eruptions on the roots. In severe attacks crops do not grow well and roots or tubers are small. If severe, fumigate the soil with Nemagon, but with slight attacks, just use more compost or animal manure as this helps to keep the eelworm population down to reasonable proportions.

Onion Thrips: Small yellow insects which suck the leaves of onions, giving them a white spotted appearance. The centre leaves are twisted and distorted and the outer ones turn brown. This pest is almost universal and is the cause of many failures in onion crops. The thrip is minute. It is very often found in between the leaf bases. The spots caused by the damage to the tissue start by being very small indeed, but as feeding continues they rapidly enlarge, by which time the damage is done. As they are so difficult to see in the early stages, it is best to assume they are present,

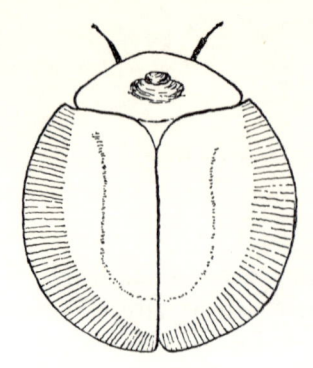

Fig. 30. Tortoise Beetle (approx. ⅜ inch)

and dust young seedlings with DDT, BHC or Malathion as soon as they are transplanted, and then every ten days. Thrips lower yields to sometimes as much as a quarter of what they should be, bulbs will be small and often the plant will die down prematurely.

COMMON DISEASES OF TUBERS, ROOTS AND BULBS

Potato Blight: The Irish potato is very susceptible to this disease in the more humid regions. The fungus first attacks the leaves, causing brown, rapidly spreading patches of dead tissue. Eventually all the foliage looks dead and the plant may die down completely. If plants are attacked when young the tuber formation will be arrested and the yield small. There is a danger too of spores being washed into the soil and attacking the tubers, making them useless. A preventive spray is better than waiting for an attack. It is usually enough to spray with Bordeaux Mixture every 10 days. Spray only on dry days: the residue will dry on the leaves and make a protective covering.

Potato Virus Diseases: Mosaic virus produces a light green or yellowish mottling on the leaves. It is often spread by aphids and usually results in lower yields. Plant only tubers from stocks known to be free from the disease and spray against aphids.

Leaf-Roll virus makes lower leaves roll inwards towards the mid-rib and the plants look abnormally upright in habit. A slight rolling of the younger leaves should not be regarded as a symptom of this disease. The disease is transmitted by aphids. Use the same treatment as that already given for Mosaic virus.

Leaf Spot in Sweet Potatoes: Can be recognised from brown bordered white spots scattered over the leaves. It is not serious and control measures are not necessary.

Downy Mildew on Onions: Affected leaves show a purplish fungus growth just below the tip, and they later turn yellow and die. The bulbs of plants affected do not reach top size. Under high rainfall or during heavy dews, this can be serious; fungus spores can remain in the soil and affect a subsequent crop. All affected leaves and trash should be burnt. Spray affected plants with Zineb or a Zineb compound.

Pink Rot of Onions: The roots of affected plants wither and turn pink. New roots will be produced, but these will suffer the same fate, with the result that bulbs will not attain good size. Do not grow onions on this soil for five years, and use varieties which appear to have some resistance to the disease.

Leaf Blight in Carrot: Most serious where conditions are humid. The ends of affected leaves turn brown, wither and die, and roots therefore do not attain a good size. Bordeaux Mixture will help, but it is better not to grow carrots at the most humid period of the year.

V. THE LEAF AND STEM VEGETABLES

It is from the vegetables in this section that the home gardener will probably get the most satisfaction.

The freshness of leaf vegetables is of paramount importance, as they lose much of their value if allowed to wilt. Nearly all of them are a rich source of the most important vitamins, particularly those which can be eaten raw. Leaf vegetables contain many of the mineral salts which are so necessary to us; watercress, among others, is particularly high in iron, and iron is often in short supply in tropical diets.

When growing these crops, it is best to try to assess first of all what will be needed of each particular crop, so that too much is not ready at one time. To get maximum benefit, it is best to make small plantings at regular intervals throughout the planting period so that produce can be eaten when at its best.

Chapter 1 CABBAGES AND CAULIFLOWERS

CABBAGE   Brassica oleracea var. capitata

Common names: Cabbage, White-hearted cabbage.

The cabbage is of European origin and was esteemed by the Greeks and the Romans. It is now grown universally, and in many countries is regarded as one of the most important leaf vegetables.

If the correct variety is used it can be grown under a very wide range of conditions. Although generally it grows best under medium, well-distributed rainfall, some varieties will produce good heads under heavy rainfall of 90 inches a year. Varieties producing the larger-sized heads do better at the higher altitudes, and those producing smaller heads do better at the lower. All cabbage prefer a slightly acid soil, but most tropical soils with a pH lower than 4·5 will need an addition of lime.

At the lower altitudes plantings made at the onset of the rains will give the best results, while in the highlands those planted at the end of the rains do well.

SUITABLE VARIETIES	LOW AND MEDIUM ALTITUDES	HIGH ALTITUDES
Conical or pointed hearts	Jersey Wakefield Charleston Wakefield Early Offenham	Winningstadt
Round hearts	Copenhagen Market Golden Acre	
Flat-round hearts	Succession	Early Drumhead

Cabbages need a deep rich soil for quick growth. Beds should be double-dug and limed where necessary. Use compost or animal manure at the rate of 2 bushels per 100 square feet and a good mixed fertiliser at 1 lb. the same area for rich soils: use 2 lbs. of fertiliser for the same area in poor soils. Fork in to the top soil and then mulch to conserve moisture.

It is best to plant the seed in seedboxes, using the usual mixture (see page 27). Sow in drills not more than $\frac{1}{2}$ inch deep and cover with fine soil. The more thinly the seeds are sown in the drills the better: the seedlings are easier to transplant, the danger of 'damping-off' in the seedbox is minimised and the plants are more robust. Water the young seedlings frequently, but do not let the soil in the box get soggy and waterlogged.

Transplant to the beds after about a month, when the seedlings should be about 4 inches high. Before transplanting, water the seedbox well so that as much soil as possible will stick to the roots and there will be no check to plant growth. Remove each one separately; never pull them, as this ruins the feeding roots and the seedlings will be severely checked. Space them 18 inches apart in the rows, 3 rows to a bed for varieties with smaller heads and 2 rows for the larger ones.

Since the seedlings will in all probability be attacked by insects whilst still young, it is advisable to place a metal or bamboo collar round each one as they are planted; don't let the mulch come right up to the collar. By the time the plant has grown higher than the collar the danger will have lessened, but the collars can remain until the crop is harvested.

Quick growth is essential and water should be given as required. If a top dressing of mixed fertiliser, or preferably sulphate of ammonia or nitrate of soda, is applied in about a month, this will make for rapid growth. If using either of the two latter, do not let it get on the leaves as it may burn them. An application of 1 lb. per bed given in a ring round each plant should be sufficient.

The smaller-headed varieties mature in about 2 months; the larger ones need another month.

In low-lying humid areas it is difficult to get the plants to form a tight heart. In this case, do not leave them in the hope that a tight heart will form later, but use them whilst they are young.

A planting of one bed a month throughout the planting season should produce enough for the average family when used with other types of leaf vegetable.

COLLARD   *Brassica oleracea* var. *acephala*

Common names: Collard, Kitchen green.

This grows far better than cabbage at the lower altitudes as it is far more tolerant of the humid conditions which often maintain in the wet coastal belt. It does not produce a heart, but is similar in all other respects to cabbage. It has one further advantage at lower altitudes, which is that it will produce good seed—very important where good seed is hard to get.

Treat collard in the same way as cabbage, 3 rows to a bed. The leaves can either be harvested separately, a few from each plant as required, or the whole head can be taken. In the former case, take out flower shoots as they appear; once the plant produces flowers there will be no more green leaves.

SCOTCH KALE   *Brassica oleracea* var. *fimbriata*

Common names: Scotch Kale, Scotch Curled Kale.

This variety of the cabbage family does not heart either and again does well under most conditions. The leaves are apt to be more fibrous than collard, and for this reason are little affected by insects. This makes it suitable for parts where insects are a nuisance.

In all respects, treat in the same way as collard. The leaves are usually harvested separately. They can be cut from three months after planting and will continue for a further two months, or even longer.

COUVE TRONCHUDA *Brassica oleracea* var. *tronchuda*

Common names: Couve Tronchuda, Portuguese cabbage.

A low-growing, non-heading type, with prominent mid-ribs to the leaves which are much esteemed. Only grows well at the higher altitudes. Do not consider for the lower altitudes, except some distance from the equator.

Treat in the same way as cabbage, but give a top dressing of fertiliser a month after transplanting.

The mid-ribs are used in the same way as Sea Kale and have a pleasant and distinctive taste.

CELERY CABBAGE *Brassica pekinensis*

Common names: Celery cabbage, Chinese cabbage, Pe-Tsai, Wong-Bak.

A delicately flavoured vegetable which, while it only grows to perfection in the highlands, is worth trying at the lower altitudes. At the lower altitudes the leaves do not clasp together quite as tightly as they should so that the inner leaves are not well blanched, but it will still be very good to eat. Under good conditions the cabbage grows to as much as 2 feet high, but below 1,000 feet 18 inches is usual.

Grow as for cabbage but spaced more widely apart. As it needs quick growth, give a dressing of fertiliser a month after planting out in the beds. This crop matures very quickly and harvest should start in less than 2 months. Make a delightful dish steamed and served with butter sauce.

CHINESE CABBAGE *Brassica chinensis*

Common names: Chinese cabbage, Pak-Choi.

Rather like the previous species, but this has broader smooth leaves with wide, white mid-ribs, and grows up to 20 inches. It can be grown in most places and is worth trying, even at the lower altitudes under high rainfall.

Treat in the same way as cabbage, with the wider spacing, and give a top dressing of fertiliser about a month after transplanting. Harvested about 2 months after planting and used in the same way as the previous species.

Fig. 31. *left:* Celery Cabbage   *right:* Chinese Cabbage

KOHL-RABI *Brassica oleracea* var. *gongylodes*

Common names: Kohl-Rabi, Kohl-Kohl, Turnip cabbage.

This useful vegetable can be grown at all altitudes and under all levels of rainfall, but it prefers lower rainfall. Sandy soils are best, but with good drainage most soil types are suitable.

The short-swollen stem is used in the same way as a turnip, which makes it an excellent substitute where turnip does not flourish.

Drill the seed direct into the bed, previously enriched with fertiliser at 1 lb. per 100 square feet, forked into the soil. Drill thinly. Only 2 drills can be accommodated in a 4-foot wide bed. Thin out later to leave only one plant every 10 inches along the row.

The thickened stems should be harvested when about 3 inches in diameter. They become fibrous and sometimes pungent if left to stand longer. In planning the planting, allow $1\frac{1}{2}$ months from sowing to harvest.

SUITABLE VARIETIES
Earliest White   Early White Vienna

CAULIFLOWER *Brassica oleracea* var. *botrytis*

This vegetable has probably given more headaches to tropical gardeners than any other. But many of the failures are due to the fact that the importance of getting the correct variety and planting at the right time has not been appreciated.

Unlike the cabbage, the cauliflower cannot tolerate a very acid soil, and lime must be applied where the pH is below pH 5·0. It is intolerant, too, of deficiencies of boron and some other elements. Provided the right variety is used, it will grow from sea level right up to the highlands. 'Early Patna' is good for the lower altitudes, and 'Early Snowball' for medium and highlands. It does best under medium rainfall, but grows quite well under heavy rains if drainage is satisfactory.

The best results will be obtained from plantings made during the dry season as long as strict attention is given to watering at all stages. The seeds must be planted in seedboxes or baskets, and in the usual mixture (see page 27). Drill thinly, so that the young plants will have plenty of room. One very successful method with cauliflowers is to transplant the seedlings into another seedbox, spaced 2 inches apart each way, and eventually when they are 4 to 5 inches high, out into the beds. It is essential that seedlings planted out into the beds must be strong and healthy: weaker ones will not do well. Whilst in the seedboxes, do not shade the seedlings more than is absolutely necessary, or they will be drawn to the light and be spindly.

Plant the seedlings in the bed in the same way as cabbage. First double-dig and lime, if necessary, later giving compost or animal manure at

2 bushels per 100 square feet. Do not apply fertiliser because this tends to make excessive leaf growth, with small leaves sometimes being formed in the 'curd' or flower.

It is thought advisable to tie the leaves loosely together as soon as a curd is formed so that it will be protected from the weather. If this is done, watch the plants carefully during heavy rains as water trapped inside the leaves can easily rot the curd.

'Early Patna' should produce good curds within 7 weeks of transplanting, and 'Early Snowball' from 9 to 10 weeks.

It is better to make a succession of small plantings during the dry season at monthly intervals, rather than one large planting.

SPROUTING BROCCOLI *Brassica oleracea* var. *italica*

This type produces 'curds' similar but smaller than those of the cauliflower, with still smaller flowering shoots from the leaf axils. At the lower altitudes flowers are not formed, but the young shoots make a very tasty vegetable. At the higher altitudes, excellent purple curds are produced at the head and from the leaf axils.

It can be grown under high rainfall and in acid soils, and is best planted at the onset of the rains, using the planting method already described for cauliflower. Young shoots can be harvested 3 months after planting, and will continue for about 2 months.

SUITABLE VARIETY
Sutton's 'Purple Sprouting'.

Chapter 2   THE SPINACHES

ENGLISH SPINACH   Spinacia oleracea

An annual from south-western Asia, which is grown mainly in temperate America and in Europe, but which can be grown in the tropics at the higher altitudes. It is not drought resistant, and though it will do well on the sandier soils if there is sufficient moisture, it is best on the richer loams. It will not tolerate an acid soil and most soils should therefore be limed.

It is best planted at the coolest season of the year as the crop cannot stand hot, dry conditions. Two plantings made at different times during this period should give an abundance of green leaves.

Give the beds at least 2 bushels of compost per 100 square feet, and sow thinly in drills, 2 rows to a bed.

Young shoots or leaves can be picked after $1\frac{1}{2}$ months, and this can continue as long as the plants do not flower.

NEW ZEALAND SPINACH   Tetragonia expansa

A low-growing, trailing plant from Australia and New Zealand, which grows quite successfully during the cooler months, from about 1,000 feet upwards. It is fairly tolerant of dry conditions and can be grown on most soils.

Drill the seeds direct into the beds, one drill down the centre of a 4-foot wide bed. Two months after planting, thin the seedlings to leave one good plant every 2 feet. The leaves and young shoots can be gathered as required from 3 months after sowing, and will continue for a long period as long as the flowers are removed as soon as they appear.

INDIAN SPINACH   Basella alba and B. rubra

Common names: Indian spinach, Country spinach, Malabar nightshade.

This succulent vine from Asia, Africa and tropical America is widely known, and is extremely useful for growing in the lower and more humid parts. In order to make rapid succulent growth, it needs a soil rich in humus. It is tolerant of acid conditions. There are two species which, apart from the colour of leaves and stems, are identical—*B. alba* is bright green and *B. rubra* has a reddish tinge.

Incorporate as much compost as possible into the beds, together with an application of at least 1 lb. of sulphate of ammonia or a good mixed fertiliser.

Plant the seed at the onset of the rains direct to the bed, 2 feet apart in the rows, with 2 rows to a 4-foot wide bed. Heavily mulch the bed to conserve moisture.

As it is a trailing plant, the best results are obtained when it is allowed to trail over a framework erected over the bed. Fix the framework about a foot above the surface of the bed. One made of bamboo or the ribs of palm fronds is suitable. With this support the foliage will avoid a lot of the dirt thrown about from soil splashings.

The first leaves can be harvested 6 weeks after sowing, and during the rains harvest can continue for several months. Flower stems soon appear at the leaf axils and these must be removed or the production of leaves will diminish.

This is a valuable and easily-grown leaf crop which should be included in all gardens in humid, low-lying parts. One bed should be enough for the average family.

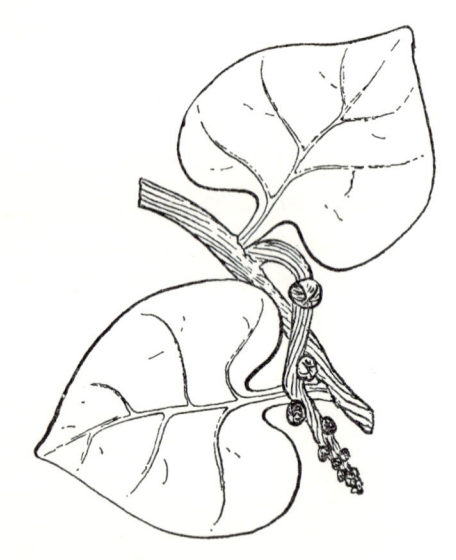

Fig. 32. Indian Spinach

AFRICAN SPINACH *Amaranthus caudatus, A. tricolor* and *A. spinsus*

In the tropics people are inclined to consider this a poor leaf vegetable, but it is in fact surprisingly rich dietetically. It grows well at the lower altitudes under heavy rainfall, and on the poorer sandy soils.

Plantings are usually confined to the rainy season, when the maximum leaf growth is obtained. Either drill or scatter the seed broadcast over the bed and cover lightly with fine soil. If broadcast, sow fairly thickly, and a month later thin out and use the thinnings in the kitchen. Leave roughly one good plant every 8 inches each way. When the plants are about 1 foot high, a dressing of compost or fertiliser will promote faster growth. Soon after this leaves can be harvested, or the young shoots cut as soon as they appear at the leaf axils. Flower stalks should be removed as soon as they appear.

CHARD *Beta vulgaris* var. *cicla*

Common names: Chard, Swiss Chard, Spinach beet.

This near relative of the beetroot produces an abundance of broad, oval leaves which may be anything up to 12 inches in length. It grows at all altitudes, but gives a greater yield in the cooler highlands. It tolerates high rainfall conditions, but can also be grown in drier areas if watered. Responds well to compost and fertiliser. One of the most suitable varieties is 'Lucullus'.

Seeds are drilled direct to the beds from the onset of the rains until the middle of the rainy season. Give the beds a liberal dressing of compost or animal manure—2 bushels per 100 square feet at least and 1 lb. of mixed fertiliser, forked into the top soil.

Drill the seeds as thinly as possible so that when the seedlings are about 3 inches high, few will be wasted in thinning. Leave one good plant every 8 inches along the row.

The leaves are gathered singly from the plants and they are ready to pick about 2 months after sowing. The harvest period depends largely on location and the richness of the soil; a minimum of a month can be expected, but under good conditions several months can be counted upon.

Chapter 3   LETTUCE, ENDIVE AND CRESS

LETTUCE   Lactuca sativa

In ancient times the Hebrews used lettuce in the Passover Ritual and considered it a sacred plant. The Romans used it as an appetiser, dressing it as a salad, and this has continued to be its main use to the present day. The Latin name, *Lactuca*, indicates the milky juice which exudes from the stem when it is cut. It is one of the most widely grown of the salad crops and, as long as the right variety is chosen, can be grown throughout the tropics.

Lettuce does not like a very acid soil, nevertheless its tolerance of soils is surprising because it will grow on most, as long as they are enriched with compost and fertiliser to support rapid growth.

There are three botanical varieties of interest to the gardener, and as each requires different conditions, it is important to choose the right one for your particular area.

The Head, or Butterhead (*L. sativa* var. *capitata*) produces leaves soft and oily in texture. Under best conditions it will produce a tight heart. It should not be grown where rains are heavy as the foliage damages easily. Grows well under medium rainfall, and during the dry season if well watered. At the lower altitudes the following varieties are good: 'Mignonette', 'Golden Ball'.

The Leaf, Crisp or Curled (*L. sativa* var. *crispa*) produces large, tougher leaves, which are twisted to form a loose heart, and the edges are crimped and cut. This lettuce is best for high rainfall conditions as it does not damage easily. It will grow superbly at all seasons in the highlands. Good varieties are Sutton's 'A.1.', Webb's 'Wonderful'.

The Cos or Romaine (*L. sativa* var. *longifolia*) is only suitable from 2,000 feet upwards as it rapidly runs to seed lower down. Good varieties are Sutton's 'Superb', Lobjoit's 'Green Cos'.

On the beds use a minimum of 2 bushels of compost per 100 square feet, but twice this amount can be given efficiently. Mixed fertiliser at 1 lb. for the same area is also necessary.

The seed is best planted in seedboxes or baskets. Scatter it very thinly over the surface and then cover with fine soil. Water after sowing and put the box in the shade, covered with a board to conserve moisture and aid germination. Lift the board each day to check on germination, and when this is observed remove the board altogether. Good seed should germinate in 5 days. Water every other day, except in dry periods when it may be necessary to water every day.

When the seedlings show 5 leaves they can be transplanted into the bed. Do this in the evening or on a dull day as wilting must be avoided. Plant the smaller Head lettuce 9 inches apart in the rows, and the larger Leaf and Cos 12 inches apart, all with 4 rows to the bed.

Quick growth is essential. A check in growth will produce leathery leaves which often have a bitter flavour. Mulch between the plants is most necessary. Except during rainy periods, they must be well watered. Test the soil to a depth of 3 inches: if it feels damp at that depth, wait another day.

A dressing of sulphate of ammonia or nitrate of soda given when the plants are about half grown will speed up growth. But be careful not to get any of it on the leaves.

Harvest as soon as some of the plants get to a reasonable size or there will be a wasteful surplus before the crop has finished. Dependent upon climate and altitude, the following are average times for the three classes:

Head: 50–60 days; Leaf: 80–90 days: Cos: 70–80 days.

Although it involves a little more work in producing seedlings in small batches, it is much better to plant half a bed every 2 or 3 weeks than make one large single planting.

ENDIVE *Cichorium endivia*

Common names: Endive, Escarolle.

Endive is grown extensively. In some tropical countries it is easier to grow than lettuce and may well become of greater importance than it is at the present. The leaves do not form a tight heart, and at the lower altitudes only a rosette of leaves is produced, but generally speaking as a salad vegetable it compares favourably with the lettuce. Many gardeners are put off by the bitter flavour, not realising that endive should be blanched. When blanched, the bitter flavour disappears.

Larger plants are produced in the highlands than at the lower levels, but even at sea level reasonable results can be obtained if grown properly. In general, conditions which suit Leaf lettuce will suit endive.

When the plants are a reasonable size, start blanching a few at a time. Place suitable pots or cans over the plants and leave them for about 7 days—though this will have to be determined by local conditions. If left too long, the plants deteriorate rapidly, so only blanch as many as can be used in a few days.

LAND CRESS *Barbarea praecox*

Common names: Land cress, American cress.

This is a valuable salad crop which is easily grown at any height above

500 feet. Unfortunately, it is not nearly well enough known. This is a pity as it is very useful in salads. It is a low-growing plant resembling Watercress (Fig. 34) and is used in the same way. Its great attraction is that it does not need running water to grow in.

It is normally treated as an annual, but it is actually a perennial and a bed once established will continue to produce for a long time. Initially it will probably have to be started from seed, but afterwards cuttings can be taken from existing plants to increase the stock.

Drill the seed direct into the bed, with 1 foot between drills. When a few inches high, thin the seedlings out to leave one good plant every 6 inches along the row. Harvest the green shoots from 2 months after sowing, and see that all flower stalks are removed as soon as they appear. The best time to sow the seed or propagate by cuttings is at the beginning of the rains, so that the plants are well established before the dry season starts. During very hot dry weather, cover the beds lightly with palm fronds, or something similar, so that the leaves do not scorch.

INDIAN CRESS   *Tropaeolum majus*

Common names: Indian cress, Nasturtium

The leaves of the common nasturtium are excellent in salad. It will grow at all altitudes, though at the lower levels it will not flower and fresh supplies of seed will have to be bought for each planting. If you do think of growing it, why not use it as a border round the garden, or along the sides of beds containing the longer-maturing vegetables. It is not an important salad crop, but it should certainly be represented by a few plants in the garden, if seed is available. Plant at the beginning of the rains and take leaves singly as required.

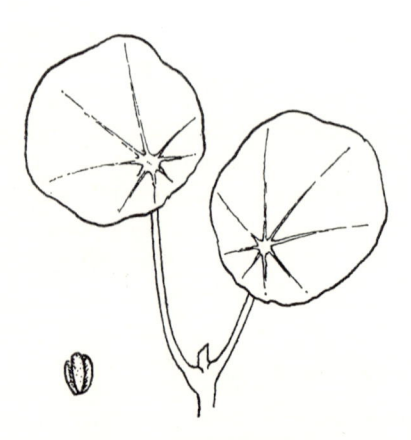

Fig. 33. Indian Cress

Fig. 34. Watercress

WATERCRESS *Rorippa Nasturtium-aquaticum*

Watercress can not only be grown satisfactorily where running water is available, but also in high rainfall areas in sunken beds. When growing in sunken beds, line the sides with clay if this is possible, so that the moisture can be retained. In these conditions it is difficult to bring the plants through the dry season, even when watered well, but still well worth trying. In the highlands there is usually a plentiful supply of running water, and this should be used. But first make sure that no transmissible diseases are present in the water because these could make the green shoots dangerous to eat.

The crop is propagated either by seeds or cuttings; sow the seed in low-lying ground which can be watered. When the seedlings are large enough to transplant, put them by the side of a stream and make a barrier round the plot so that they are not washed away.

Give shade during the dry season and, like all the leaf vegetables, remove the flower stalks as soon as they appear.

Chapter 4   OTHER INTERESTING LEAF AND STEM VEGETABLES

CELERY   *Apium graveolens*

The myth that good crisp celery cannot be grown in the tropics through lack of frost, has long been exploded. It can be grown at all except the lowest altitudes, as long as the right variety is used and it receives the right treatment. In the highlands, the longer-stalked varieties such as 'Giant White' and 'Clayworth Pink' give good results, whilst lower down 'Golden Self-blanching' is best.

Celery needs ample moisture to promote quick growth and should therefore be planted at the onset of the rains. In order to further conserve the moisture, grow the plants in trenches dug in the beds, 1 foot deep and 1 foot wide. Put compost to a depth of at least 3 inches in the bottom of the trench and cover with a similar layer of good top soil.

Fig. 35. Celery

It is best to plant the seeds in boxes or baskets, filled with the usual mixture. Sow thinly in drills across the box and then cover with a fine layer of soil. Water and then cover with a board. Check for germination daily and remove the board as soon as the first seedlings appear. The young plants grow slowly and will remain in the seedbox for up to 6 weeks, hence the need to sow thinly in the drills.

When they show 4 to 5 leaves, transplant into the trench, spaced 8 inches apart along the centre. Water well after transplanting and shade from hot sun. When 6 inches high, give a top dressing of either sulphate of ammonia or nitrate of soda, using 1 lb. for 50 feet of trench. Take care none gets on the leaves.

At the lower altitudes the plants tend to form a flat rosette of leaves, but this can be cured by tying them up loosely to form a bunch. As the plants grow, gradually move the soil up around each one to blanch the stems. This can be done in 3 stages, the final stage being $2\frac{1}{2}$ months after transplanting. Once the final moulding has been made, the plants must be used within a few days or they may start to rot at the heart. Do only a few plants at a time—enough for your requirements—so that none are lost in this way.

CELERIAC   *Apium graveolens* var. *rapaceum*

Common names: Celeriac, Turnip-rooted celery.

Similar to celery, except that the upper part of the root and the lower part of the stem swells to form the edible part of the plant. It has the same flavour as celery and is used as a substitute in soups, or as a cooked vegetable.

It is usually only successful above 3,000 feet under medium rainfall, but it has been grown with reasonable results at the lower levels. Culture is the same as that for celery. It will be ready to harvest in about 4 months.

PURSLANE   *Portulaca oleracea*

Common names: Purslane, Pigweed, Wild Portulaca.

A low-growing succulent plant suited for growing at the lowest altitudes and under heavy rainfall. Under these conditions where at certain seasons

Fig. 36. Purslane

there may well be a shortage of green vegetables, this little plant can serve well. The spatula-shaped green or reddish-brown leaves are produced over a long period, and once established the plant will usually seed itself.

WATER LEAF *Talinum triangulare*

This small, fleshy herb originated in South America, and is now well known through most of the tropics. The narrow, blunt-tipped leaves are more or less succulent.

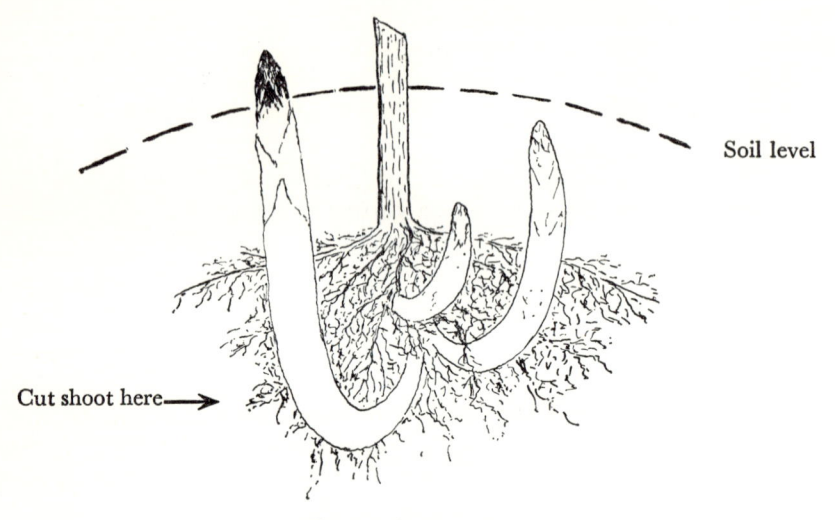

Fig. 37. Asparagus

Like Purslane, it is easy to grow, is more suited to the lower altitudes and tolerates heavy rainfall. Broadcast the seed over the bed and cover thinly with fine soil. The young shoots can be harvested in about 6 weeks, and will continue for some time.

ASPARAGUS *Asparagus officinalis* var. *altilis*

This should not be overlooked by the keen gardener. It can be grown at all altitudes in the tropics and, with a little trouble, will produce excellent shoots. There are a number of varieties available, many of which have not been tried out in the tropics. One of the very old ones gives good results, 'Mary Washington'. In some countries 2-year old roots can be had from market gardeners, and these should be used in preference to seed; it takes rather longer to get results from seed.

However, seed is probably what you will have to use. Double-dig the bed and incorporate into it 4 bushels of compost per 100 square feet.

Bring the top soil to a fine tilth and make 2 drills along the bed, 2 feet apart. Do not make the drills any more than 1 inch deep. Scatter the seed very thinly. Cover with fine soil and water.

When the seedlings are about 6 inches high, thin out, leaving a strong plant every 8 inches. If the thinnings are taken up carefully, they can be used in another bed. Leave the plants to flower and allow them to die down before cutting off the foliage. The roots will now lie dormant until the next growing season. Some time before the next season heap compost along the line of the rows to a depth of at least 6 inches. This will provide sufficient food to produce the next season's shoots.

Just after the beginning of the rains, young green tips will begin to appear through the compost. Harvest them as they appear by gently moving the compost from around them until the whole white shoot is revealed as it emerges from the main root ball. Take care not to damage any adjacent shoots which have not yet appeared above ground. The harvest will not be large in the first season and *some shoots must be left on each plant* so that they can grow and produce leaves: if none were left, the plant would die. Those left on the plant can be allowed to flower, and then cut back as in the first year. Again, the beds must be given a good dressing of compost to encourage the next year's growth of shoots.

Commercial growers consider that the male plants produce more shoots than the female, so remove the latter and substitute male plants at the end of the season. Established asparagus beds will continue to yield for many years if given enough compost each year, plus a dressing of common salt, 1 lb. for 25 feet, every other year.

Chapter 5 PESTS AND DISEASES OF THESE CROPS

Aphids: Can be serious, especially in the Brassica crops, where they are apt to congregate in the folds of the leaves. It is advisable to use Rotenone dust as this is not toxic to humans. Nicotine sulphate can be used, and it is effective, but it must not be applied near to harvest time.

Caterpillars and Loopers: More serious on the Brassica crops than others in this section. DDT may be used on young plants, but not within 14 days of harvest.

Grasshoppers: Both the common green, and the variegated yellow and green types, can be a menace on leaf crops. Chlordane dust can be used on the Brassica crops. but not within 30 days of harvest. Hand picking may have to be restored to rather than use highly poisonous preparations on these crops.

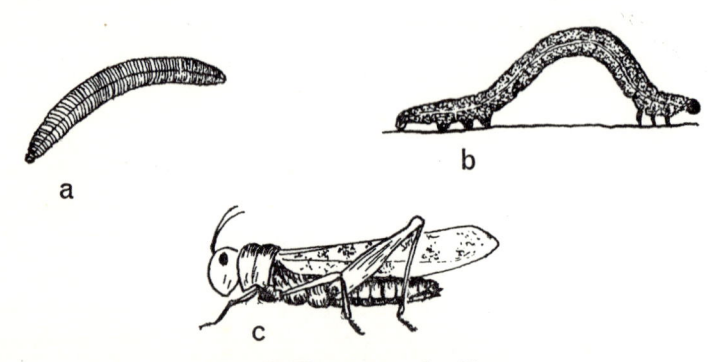

Fig. 38. Three pests of cabbage
(*a*) larva; (*b*) Looper (approx. $1\frac{1}{2}$–2 inches); (*c*) Grasshopper (approx. 2 inches)

Cutworms: The larvae of many species of moth. They hatch out from eggs laid on the stems or leaves of crop plants, or others nearby, and spend the day time under the mulch, under rubbish, or in the soil. Some of them are very large – up to $2\frac{1}{2}$ inches and thick and juicy. They attack the stem both above and under the soil, and often the damage causes death. Mix chlordane into the top soil as a fumigant.

Nematodes: Boil-like eruptions containing eelworms. Once they get on plant roots the plant will not thrive. Burn all affected roots and use more compost. In serious cases, fumigate the soil with a soil fumigant, such as Nemagon.

COMMON DISEASES OF THE LEAF CROPS

Nutritional disorders: The cauliflower is usually most seriously affected, as it has specific requirements of some elements. The syptoms of boron deficiency are easy to recognise. When the stem is cut through it will be hollow and brown and there will also be a browning of the 'curd'. Apply 1 oz. of borax to 30 square yards, but remember that an excess, even if caused by uneven spreading, can do more harm than good.

With a shortage of calcium, cauliflower leaves become thin and whip-like—hence the common name for this condition, 'Whip-tail'. Apply 1 lb. of lime per 100 square feet, or spray the plants with a special calcium spray.

Black Rot in Brassica Crops: A bacterial disease which can be seed-borne. Most good commercial seed houses sell disease-free or treated seed. It is easily recognised. In the leaves the edge, usually at the tip, turns yellow in a wide V, and sometimes they are distorted and growth is poor. If the stem is cut through a characteristic black ring will be seen where the bacteria has attacked the tissues.

Do not grow any of the Brassica family on affected land for at least three years, and make sure that you buy treated or disease-free seed.

Damping-off in Seedlings: Can be recognised by a fine cobweb-like fungus around the stems of seedlings at soil level, which eventually causes the plant to wilt and later die. It can be particularly bad if seedlings are over-crowded in the seedboxes, hence the advice that seedlings should be sown thinly. Excess shading will also cause damping-off.

Where this occurs, treat future seed with Semesan before planting. If Semesan is not available, spray seedlings as soon as they emerge with Cheshunt Compound (see page 32) and repeat every two weeks.

Downy Mildew in Lettuce: A fungus disease which can cause trouble when heavy night mists are prevalent. Pale yellowish areas appear on the leaves, which, on the opposite side of the patches, are covered with a downy fungus. Spreads rapidly. Some control can be obtained by preventive spraying with Bordeaux Mixture when the plants are half grown. If a small outbreak occurs, harvest and use the effected plants, taking off the diseased leaves and burning them.

VI. CULINARY HERBS

Fresh herbs add much to the appearance and flavour of many dishes but their use in the kitchen is so often restricted because they are not grown locally or their retail price is so high.

Thirteen of the most widely known of these herbs are described below. Of these all except ginger and garlic, are at their best when used fresh and to keep a small plot containing some of them will be very worthwhile. As only small plantings should be made, one bed will usually be sufficient to hold quite a collection. Where a long dry season is experienced some plants can be plotted up and grown in the cooler conditions of the verandah where they can be put amongst the flowering pot plants.

Chapter 1

BASIL (SWEET)   *Ocimum basilicum*

An annual herb from tropical Asia, Africa and the Pacific Islands. The leaves have a delightfully aromatic scent and are at their best when used fresh with salads. Sweet Basil will grow well at all altitudes and under most conditions.

Plant the seed at the beginning of the rains in seedboxes, and transplant into the beds when about two inches high at a spacing of 10 inches apart, each way. The leaves can be harvested within a month of planting out, a few being taken from each plant at a time. The small bushes will soon send up flower shoots and these must be removed otherwise no further young shoots and leaves will be produced. One plant may be allowed to flower to provide a supply of seeds for next season. It is as well to pot up a few plants towards the end of the rains and grow them through the dry season in the verandah or on a windowsill as the plants cannot stand very dry conditions.

Sweet Basil is regarded by many as the most fragrant of all herbs. It is used with cheese, egg dishes, spaghetti, potatoes and sauces when fresh, and in casseroles, soups and stews when dried. Try a little chopped up over freshly sliced tomatoes.

CHERVIL   *Anthriscus cerefolium*

A small annual herb, native of Europe, which looks very similar to parsley, the leaves being used mainly for garnishing. It prefers a sandy soil, and only grows successfully in the highlands.

Plant the seed in a seedbox at the beginning of the rains. The bed should be well prepared and compost and fertiliser added. Plant out the seedlings when they are about 3 inches high at a spacing of 6 inches, each way. The leaves will be ready to pick from two months after transplanting and should be taken while still young as they tend to become tough if left to mature.

In flavour chervil combines those of parsley and fennel and is more aromatic than either. Its main use is for garnishing but it is also used with other herbs for seasoning. The curled-leaf type is to be preferred which is used only for garnishing.

Fig. 39. (*a*) Sage; (*b*) Seed head of Dill; (*c*) Bulbous stem of Fennel; (*d*) *Fine curled* Parsley; (*e*) *Plain* Parsley; (*f*) Sweet Basil

CHIVES *Allium schoenoprasum*

A member of the onion family which can be grown at all altitudes. The small bulbs are of milder flavour than most onions, a point in their favour with many people.

If chives are not grown in your area it will be necessary to start with seed. Later, when you have established plants, the clumps of bulbs can be separated and the individual bulbs planted out to increase the stock.

The seed is sown in a seedbox at the beginning of the rains, using the same method as already described for planting onions. The young seedlings can either be transplanted into the herb bed or used along the side of the bed away from the sun or a bed which has tall vegetables as these will give the chives the shade they require. Plant the seedlings 9 inches apart and mulch round them well.

The gathering of the leaves can start about two months after transplanting, taking only a leaf from each plant until the plants have attained a reasonable size. The leaves are used as a garnish and also in omelets, soups, salads and stews.

There may be difficulty in keeping the plants growing through the dry season unless they are given sufficient water, mulched well and shaded.

DILL *Peucedanum graveolens*

A small, easily grown annual herb originating from Europe, having aromatic leaves and seeds. It will thrive at all altitudes above 500 feet and can be grown under medium to heavy rainfall.

The seed is drilled in seedboxes towards the middle of the rains so that the seed will ripen on the plants during the dry season. Transplant the seedlings to another seedbox when they are about 2 inches high, giving a spacing of 2 inches apart. Finally the plants, when about 4 inches high can be transplanted into the herb bed. At all times provide some shade as dill does not like full sun.

The young leaves can be harvested as required and used as a garnish for potatoes, or in meat and fish dishes, sauces and salads. The ripe seeds should be fully dried on the plant and the whole head removed with care. The whole seed head can be stored in a screwtop jar or the seeds can be threshed out and stored in the same way.

FENNEL (SWEET) *Foeniculum vulgare*

Common names: Sweet fennel, Finnochio, Florentine fennel.

A short lived perennial from Europe which should be treated as an annual when grown in the tropics. The thick, clasping stem bases which resemble bulbs, make an excellent anise-flavoured vegetable, highly prized in Italy and throughout the Mediterranean.

It is easily grown, thriving at most altitudes and under widely differing rainfall. To promote quick growth so that the stems do not become fibrous, a rich soil is necessary.

The seed is drilled thinly direct into the bed, the seedlings being later thinned to leave one good plant every foot along the row.

The bulbous stem bases will be ready to harvest about $3\frac{1}{2}$ months after planting. They can be cooked like celery or eaten raw in salads but for the latter it is better to blanch them. The ripe seeds are used in confectionary, being aromatic with a spicy flavour resembling nutmeg.

GARLIC *Allium sativum*

Common names: Garlic, Ail, Aglio.

It is not perhaps generally appreciated that garlic can be grown in most places in the tropics with may be the possible exception of the very low altitudes. The flavour and strong odour of garlic is repugnant to some people but fortunately many like it.

Garlic is normally propagated by dividing the mature bulb into its separate sections which are commonly called 'cloves'. Plant the cloves at the middle of the rainy season so that the bulbs will mature in the drier months. They should be planted 9 inches apart in the row, with the tip of the bulb just showing above ground. A sandy, well-drained soil is best but they will grow on most soil types except heavy clay.

The bulbs are harvested after the foliage has completely died down, usually about six months after planting. They should be stored in a dry place and if well sun-dried they will keep for some months. The cloves can be used to flavour salads, sauces, sausages, casseroles, soups and stews.

GINGER *Zingiber officinale*

Common names: Ginger, Jamaica ginger.

Ginger is well known both as a preserve and a condiment. It is grown throughout the tropics up to an altitude of about 3,000 feet, the best yields probably being obtained at between 500 to 1,000 feet. It will tolerate high rainfall but will do better under medium rainfall, well distributed. A rich soil is very necessary. Plantings should be made at the beginning of the rains.

It is propagated by dividing the rhizome into pieces and planting them 6 inches deep with a foot between plants in the row and $1\frac{1}{2}$ feet between rows. Shoots should appear about three weeks after planting. The rhizomes take from 9 to 10 months to mature, usually just after the foliage has died down.

For dried ginger, the roots must be fully mature and after lifting they must be washed and dried in the sun, sometimes peeled and then ground.

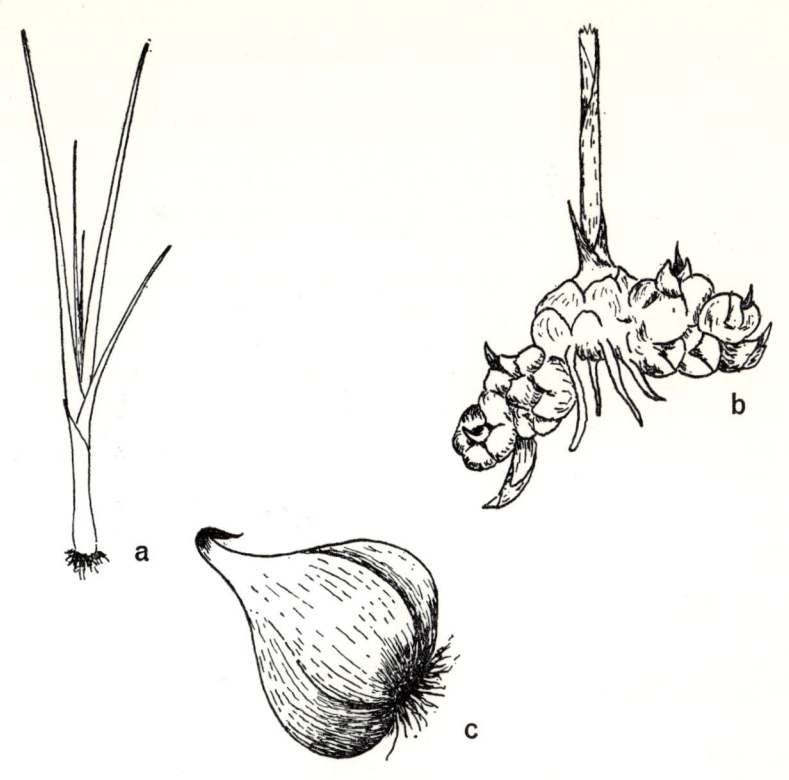

Fig. 40. (*a*) Chive; (*b*) Ginger; (*c*) Garlic

'Green' ginger is prepared from roots which, although fully grown, are not ripe. These are peeled and then boiled in sugar and water.

MARJORAM (SWEET)   *Origanum majorana*

A small shrub from North Africa having oblong-oval green leaves which are pungent, aromatic and slightly bitter. It is not widely grown but will usually do well at all altitudes and in most soils.

Plant the seed in boxes at the beginning of the rains, scattering it over the surface of the soil and covering with fine sand. Transplant the seedlings when about two inches high into the herb bed or into pots.

The green leaves are used sparingly with meats, stews, poultry and fish dishes. They can also be used when dried but some of the flavour is lost in drying.

MINT   *Mentha spicata*

A spreading, semi-prostrate herb from Europe having dark green, oval, aromatic leaves. It can be grown at all altitudes but needs great care below 500 feet and under heavy rainfall. Plants must be given shade as they cannot stand full sun.

The plant is propagated by pieces of the underground stems which readily form roots at the nodes. They should be planted in a shallow trench 2 inches deep and covered with good soil. New growth will appear after about three weeks and the young shoots can be harvested as required.

A fungus disease, Mint Rust, may attack plants and is recognised by light yellow spots appearing on the leaves and stems, the latter becoming deformed. Later the spots darken to deep brown, the leaves dry out and the plant appears to have died. For minor attacks dust with sulphur. For a severe attack the plants will have to be lifted, the roots washed in cold water and then plunged into hot water (105° to 115°F) for 10 minutes. The roots must then be planted into a new bed.

PARSLEY *Petroselinum crispum*

A very popular biennial herb, originally from Europe and grown now in almost all countries. With care it can be grown at all altitudes, but is happier at 2,000 feet and above. It is not easy to get good results where the rainfall is high or under very hot, dry conditions. Under the latter the plants must be shaded. A deep, rich soil is essential and the addition of compost is advisable.

There are two main types—the Curled and the Plain, the former is more widely used for garnishing and the latter for flavouring and in salads.

The seed of parsley does not seem to keep well in the tropics and fresh seed is to be preferred. The seed can either be drilled thinly direct into a well-manured bed or first into a seedbox. In either case do not plant deeper than $\frac{1}{2}$ inch. The seed may take several weeks to germinate so do not become anxious if no seedlings appear straight away.

If drilled direct into the bed, thin out the seedlings when they are about an inch high, leaving one good plant every 6 inches along the row. If grown in a seedbox, transplant at this distance. Mulch between the rows.

Pick the leaves before they are fully grown otherwise they will be rather fibrous, and do not take too many from any plant until it has become well established. At the lower altitudes the plants will continue to produce new leaves for several months but in the highlands this may extend to more than a year.

At the height of the harvest more leaves may be available than can comfortably be used, and the surplus may then be dried in the sun until 'brittle-dry' and stored in screw-top jars.

Parsley may suffer from one fungus, Leaf Blight, which produces large yellow patches on the leaves which later turn brown and die. The spores of the fungus can remain in the soil and will affect later plantings of parsley The affected plants should be dug up carefully and burned and no further. plantings made in that bed for several years.

ROSEMARY   *Rosmarinus officinalis*

A perennial shrub growing to a height of 5 feet and producing dark green leaves that have a fresh, sweet flavour. It is a lime-loving plant and therefore will not thrive on an acid soil unless a large dressing of lime is provided. Will only thrive at medium altitudes and above and likes full sun.

Rosemary can be grown from seed or cuttings taken from an established bush. Seed should be planted in a seedbox at the onset of the rains, the young seedlings being transplanted when a few inches high. The drainage of the bed must be good and it is advisable to plant out at the highest point in the garden. Cuttings of 5 to 6 inches in length may be taken at the beginning of the rains and planted to two-thirds their length in sandy soil in a shady bed.

The green leaves are used fresh with meats, fish, poultry and vegetables, the dried ones in stocks, stews, stuffings and pate.

SAGE   *Salvia officinalis*

A small shrub from Southern Europe, the ashy-green leaves being used as a flavouring. It grows best at the higher altitudes but, with care can be grown in pots or baskets at the lower levels. It is best under rather dry conditions and does not thrive on a very acid soil.

If established plants are not available locally for a supply of cuttings, it will be necessary to start from seed. These should be sown in a seedbox and later the seedlings planted out in pots, or in the highlands into the herb bed. At no time do the plants need a lot of water.

The leaves are used either fresh or dried with meats, cheese, pickles, pork and poultry.

THYME   *Thymus vulgaris*

A delightful small bush producing very small aromatic leaves. It is best when grown in the highlands but some success has been had at the lower altitudes when the plants are pot-grown. Prefers a dryer climate and an alkaline soil.

Sow the seed in a seedbox at the onset of the rains and plant out later into pots, or in the highlands in the bed. The whole stem is harvested as soon as flower buds appear and are tied in bundles and hung in the sun to dry thoroughly. When dry they should be handled with care as the small leaves easily fall. Thresh out all the leaves and store in a screw-top jar.

The dried leaves remain aromatic for a long period if properly stored. They are used with soups, stews, sauces and forcemeats. A little added to warmed butter also enhances the flavour of shell-fish and, used in the same way as a garnish for vegetables.

INDEX

African Spinach, 136
Allium cepa, 119
  cepa aggrigatum, 118
  fistulosum, 118
  porrum, 119
  sativum, 152
  schoenoprasum, 151
Amaranthus caudatus, 136
Animal manures, 19
Anthracnose, 56
  on Cucumber, 103
  on Garden Egg, 103
  on Melons, 103
  on Sweet Pepper, 103
Anthriscus cerefolium, 149
Aphids, 55 (Fig. 14), 100, 125, 146
Apium graveolens, 142
  graveolens rapaceum, 143
Arachis hypogaea, 53
Artichoke, Jerusalem, 110
Asparagus, 144–5 (Fig. 37)
Asparagus Bean, 46
Asparagus officinalis altilis, 144

Bacterial diseases, 105
Bambarra Groundnut, 53
Barbarea praecox, 139
Basella alba and B. rubra, 135
Basic slag, 22
Basil, Sweet, 149, 150 (Fig. 39)
Bean beetles, Mexican, 54, 55 (Fig. 14)
Bean Rust, 57
Beans, 38–44
Beds:
  raised bench, 23, 24 (Fig. 2)
  sunken, 23
Bees, 31 (Fig. 5)
Beetles, 54, 55 (Fig. 14), 100, 101 (Fig. 22), 125
Beetroot, **91,** 113–14
Bench beds, raised, 23, 24 (Fig. 2)
Beta vulgaris, 113
  vulgaris cicla, 137
Bitter Melon, 98 (Fig. 21), 99

Black Rot (brassicas), **96,** 147
Blight:
  carrot, 127
  potato, 126
  tomato, 103
Blood meal, 19
Blossom-end Rot (tomatoes), 104
Bonavist Bean, 49, **84**
Bone meal, 19
Bordeaux Mixture, 32
Bottle Gourd, 97
Brassica chinensis, 131
  oleracea acephala, 130
  oleracea botrytis, 133
  oleracea capitata, 129
  oleracea fimbriata, 130
  oleracea gongylodes, 133
  oleracea italica, 134
  oleracea tronchuda, 131
  pekinensis, 131
  rapa, 114

Cabbages, **93,** 129–32 (Fig. 31, 133
Cajanus indicus, 50
Calapogonium, 20
Capsicum annum, 65, 66
Carrots, 112, 113 (Fig. 25)
Caterpillars, 54, 100, 146
Cauliflower, **94,** 133–4
Celeriac, 143
Celery, 142 (Fig. 35)
Celery cabbage, 131
Centrosema, 20
Chard, 95, 137
Chayote, 75 (Fig. 18)
Chestnut Compound, 32
Chevril, 149
Chinese Artichoke, 122, 123 (Fig. 29)
Chinese cabbage, 131
Chives, 151, 153 (Fig. 40)
Chlordane, 30, 54
Cichorium endivia, 139
Citrullus vulgaris, 72
Clay soil, 15

Cluster Bean, 51, 52 (Fig. 13)
Cocozelle, 78 (Fig. 19)
Collard, **94,** 130
Colocasia esculenta, 123
Compost, 15–18
Contact poisons, 29
Couve Tronchuda, 131
Cress, 139–41
Cucumis melo, 73
  sativus, 69
  sativus anglicus, 70
Cucumbers, 69–71
  English, 70–1
  Ridge, 69–70
Culinary Herbs, 148–56
Curcubita maxima, 77
  moschata, 77
  pepo, 77
  pepo condensa, 77
Currant Tomato, 63
Cutworms, 33 (Fig. 6), 146
Cyamopsis psoralioides, 51

Damping-off, 57, 147
Daucus carota, 112
DDT, 30
Derris powder, 29
Diazinon, 30
Dill, 150 (Fig. 39), 151
Diocorea esculentum, 107
Diseases:
  Anthracnose, 56, 103
  Bacterial, 105
  Environmental, 104
  fighting against, 29–34
  Fungus, 56, 102–4
  Mildew, 56, 57, **87, 96,** 103, 127, 147
  of beans, peas and pulses, 54–7
  of leaf crops, 147
  of tomatoes, Garden Egg, peppers and gourds, 100–5
  of tubers, roots and bulbs, 126–7
  Rust, 57
  Virus, 56, 104–5

Dolichos lablab, 49
Double digging, 24–5 (Fig. 3)
Downy Mildew, 57
  on cucumbers, **87, 96,** 103
  on melons, 103
  on onions, 127
  on lettuce, 147
Dried blood, 19
Drill, how to make a, **90**

Eddo, 123
Eelworms (Nematodes), 54, **84,** 125, 147
Egyptian Onion, 118
Endive, 139
English Spinach, 135
Environmental diseases, 104

Fennel, 150 (Fig. 39), 151
Fertilisers (*see* Inorganic Manures)
Flea Beetle, 100, 101 (Fig. 22)
Foeniculum vulgare, 151
French Bean, 38
Fruit Rot (Garden Egg), 103
Fumigants, 29, 32, 34
Fungicides, 30, 32
Fungus diseases, 56, 102–4

Garden Egg, 64, **86**
Gardening tools, 11
Garlic, 152, 153 (Fig. 40)
Germination tests, 26
Ginger, 152, 153 (Fig. 40)
Glycine max, 51
Gourds, Tropical, 80, 97–9 (Fig. 21)
Grasshoppers, 146 (Fig. 38)
Green manuring, 20
Groundnut, 53
Gunmosis (on cucumber), 104

Helianthus tuberosus, 110
Herbs, 148–56
Hisbiscus esculentus, 74
Horse and cattle manure, 19
Hubbard, 78 (Fig. 20)

Indian Cress, 140 (Fig. 33)
Indian Spinach, 135, 136 (Fig. 32)
Inorganic manures, 14, 20–22
Insecticides, 12, 29
Insects:
  useful garden, 31 (Fig. 5)
  soil pests, 33 (Fig. 6)
Ipomoea batatas, 109

Jerusalem Artichoke, 110

Kohl-rabi, 133

Lacewing, 31 (Fig. 5)
Lactuca sativa, 138
Ladybird, 31 (Fig. 5)
Lagenaria siceraria, 97
Land Cress, 139–40
Leaf blight (carrots), 127
Leaf-curl (peppers), 104; (potatoes), 126
Leaf miner, **86,** 100
Leaf mould (tomato), 102
Leaf spot (peppers), 103; (sweet potatoes), 126; (tomato), 103
Leeks, 119
Lemon Grass, 23, 24 (Fig. 2)
Lettuce, 138–9
Lima Bean, 40, **82**
Lime, 15
Lime-sulphur solutions, 32
Lindane, 30
Loopers, 146 (Fig. 38)
Luffa, 97, 98 (Fig. 21)
Luffa acutangula, 97
Lycopersicon pimpinellifolium, 63

Malathion, 30
Maneb, 32
Mantis, 31 (Fig. 5)
Manure:
  green, 20
  inorganic, 14, 20–22
  organic, 14, 19–20
Marjoram, 153
Marrows, 77–9
Mealy Bugs, 100
Melonworms, 102
Melons, 72–3
Menta spicata, 153
Mexican Bean Beetle, 54, 55 (Fig. 14)
Mildew, 56, 57, 103, 127, 147
Millepede, 33 (Fig. 6)
Mint, 153–4
Mites, 55 (Fig. 14), 102
Mole Cricket, 33 (Fig. 6), 100
Momordica charantia, 99
Mosaic virus (peppers), 104; (potatoes), 126
Mucuna, 20
Mulching, 25
Mung Bean, 49
Muriate of Potash, 22
Musk Melon, 73 (Fig. 17)

Nemagon, 34, 54
Nematodes (eelworms), 54, **84,** 125, 147
New Zealand Spinach, **96,** 135
Nitrate of Ammonia, 21
  of Lime, 21
  of Potassium, 21
  of Soda, 21
Nursery shed for seed boxes, 27, 28 (Fig. 4)

Ocimun basilicum, 149
Okra, 74, **87**
Onions, 117–19, 120 (Fig. 27)
Organic manure, 14, 19–20
Origanum majorana, 153

Parathion, 30
Parsley, 150 (Fig. 39), 154
Peas, 45–8
Peppers, 65–8 (Fig. 16)
Pests and Diseases, 29–34, 54–7, 100–105, 125–7, 146–7
Petroselinum crispum, 154
Peucedanum graveolens, 151
Peuraria, 20
Phaseolus aureus, 49
  coccineus, 39
  lunatus, 40
  vulgaris, 38
Pickleworms, **86,** 102
Pigeon Pea, 50 (Fig. 11)
Pink Rot (onions), 127
Pisum sativum, 47
Plant Bug, 102
Plant Feeding, 14–22
Portulaca oleracea, 143
Potatoes, 107–8
  virus diseases of, 126
Poultry manure, 19
Powdery Mildew, 56
  on cucumbers, 103
  on melons, 103
Psophocarpus tetragonolobus, 42
Pumpkins, 77–9, 80, **89**
Purslane, 143 (Fig. 36)
Pyrethrum, 30

Radish, 115
Raphanus sativus, 115
Red Spider Mite, 55 (Fig. 14)
Red Tomato, 59
Ridge Cucumber, 69, **89**
Rorippa Nasturtium-aquaticum, 141
Rosmarinus officinalis, 155
Rosemary, 155

Rove Beetle, 31 (Fig. 5)

Sage, 150 (Fig. 39), 155
Salsify, 122 (Fig. 28)
Salvia officinalis, 155
Sandy soil, 15
Scarlet Runner Bean, 39–40 (Fig. 7)
Scorzonera, 122
Scorzonera hispanica, 122
Scotch Kale, 130
Seaweed, 19
Sechium edule, 75
Seed:
  buying, 26
  storage of, 26, 27
Seedboxes, 27–8
Serpentine Leaf Miner, 55
Shallots, 119, 120 (Fig. 127)
Sheep and goat manure, 19
Snake Gourd, 97, 98 (Fig. 21)
Soil testing, 15
Solanum tuberosum, 107
Soy Bean, 51, 52 (Fig. 12)
Splitting (tomatoes), 104
Spinach, 135–7
Spinacia oleracea, 135
Spraying equipment, 12
Sprouting Broccoli, 134

Stachys tuberfera, 122
Stink Bugs, 101 (Fig. 22), 102
Squashes, 77–8
Sulphate of Ammonia, 20–1
  of Potash, 22
Summer Scallop, 78 (Fig. 19)
Sunken beds, 23
Superphosphate, 21
Sweet Potato, 109 (Fig. 24)
  Weevil, 125
Sword Bean, 43 (Fig. 8)

Talinum triangulare, 144
Tannia, **92,** 123–4
Telfairia occidentalis, 80
Tetragonia expansa, 135
Thrips, **91,** 125
Thyme, 155
Thymus vulgaris, 155
Tomato Fruitworm, 102
Tomato Hornworm, 101 (Fig. 22), 102
Tomatoes, 59–63, **85, 88**
Tortoise Beetles, 125
Tragopogon porrifolius, 122
Trichosanthes anguina, 97
Turnip, White, 114, 115 (Fig. 26)
Tropaeolum majus, 140

Uted Pumpkin, 80

Vegetable Marrow, 77
Vigna sesquipedalis, 46
  sinensis, 45
Virus diseases, 56, 104–5
Voandzeia subterranea, 53

Watercress, 141 (Fig. 34)
Water Leaf, **92,** 144
Watermelon, 72, 73 (Fig. 17)
Welsh Onion, 118, 120 (Fig. 27)
White Grub, 33 (Fig. 6)
White Turnip, 114, 115 (Fig. 26)
Wilt disease (peppers), 105
Winged Bean, 42, **82**
Wireworm, 33 (Fig. 6)
Wood ash, 19

Xanthosoma sagittifolium, 123

Yams, 107
Yellow Crookneck, 78 (Fig. 20)

Zineb, 32
Zingiber officinale, 152